The Best Day Hikes
in the Canadian Rockies

Tim Jensen

By Tim Jensen
Graphical Illustrations by Suko
Published in Vancouver, Canada
Printed and bound in Hong Kong
For copies and/or distribution email: tim-jensen@live.com

ISBN 978-0-9864928-0-8

Many of the photographs are owned by the writer. Some of the photographs were taken by Csuri Photography (Sjoerd de Jongh) and some are used with permission or license agreement.

Disclaimer

You are responsible for your own safety. The accuracy of the information in this book is not guaranteed. Natural hazards, sudden changes in weather, animals, trail conditions, and numerous other factors add varying degrees of risk to hiking. Take all required emergency equipment with you including an official detailed map of the area and a compass. Never undertake a trail beyond your abilities. Use this book at your own risk. The author and publisher are not liable for any injuries, loss, damages or other casualties by anyone using the information in this book.

Preface

The Best Day Hikes in the Canadian Rockies presents a compelling array of day hikes to be discovered throughout Canada's best known mountain range. Although your time may be limited, allowing for just one or two hikes in each region, it can give you a genuine taste of the most beautiful treasures of the Canadian Rockies. Your experience will be truly unforgettable when combined with the sublime Parks Canada sightseeing stops along your way. While not exhaustive of all the hiking opportunities, the very best day hikes are covered by this guide.

Of course we all have our own preferences and capabilities. Your hiking experience will vary according to your personal interest, hiking distance, elevation gain, popularity of the hike, etc. Some people are attracted to absolute wilderness – something very hard to find during the summer season around the Banff and Lake Louise area – while others gravitate towards more popular areas, enjoying the periodic company of fellow hikers. If you prefer to avoid crowds, it is best to wake up early or, if at all possible, embark on longer and more strenuous hikes.

Along most trails in the Canadian Rockies, you first have to hike a few kilometres before emerging from the forested area and reaching the more rewarding viewpoints in the alpine meadows. However a number of very short but highly satisfying hikes have been included, requiring relatively limited effort to complete them.

I wish you all a safe and exhilarating time in this amazing region of beautiful Canada – my home away from home (the Netherlands being my country of origin). With extensive hiking experience throughout the world, the Canadian Rockies is, without doubt, one of the most spectacular and memorable destinations.

I would like to thank Mark, Rick, Ara, David, Lynda and fellow hikers Ben, Ellen, Lilo, Pieter, Sjoerd and Susanne for their fabulous support in making this book happen.

Tim Jensen

$$1 \text{ KM} = 0.625 \text{ MILE}$$
$$1 \text{ MILE} = 1.6 \text{ KM}$$
$$1 \text{ m} = 3.28 \text{ ft}$$
$$1 \text{ ft} = 0.3048 \text{ m}$$

The Best Day Hikes in the Canadian Rockies – Overview

Jasper & Mount Robson area

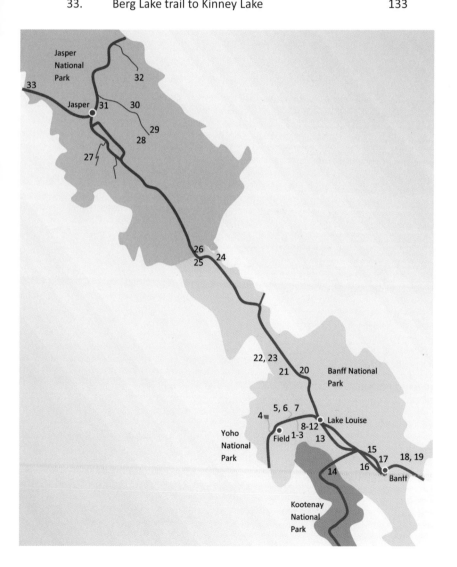

Important information

We recommend visiting a Parks Canada visitor centre prior to starting a hike. There, you can get the latest weather forecasts and other relevant information relating to trail conditions. You can also pick up reliable maps and advice. Always remember that trails can be closed at any time for a variety of reasons such as wildlife in the area, trail maintenance or physical hazards (forest fires, etc).

List of Visitor Centres:

Yoho National Park Visitor Centre
Field, Yoho National Park
Telephone: (+1) 250 343 6783
www.pc.gc.ca/yoho

Banff Visitor Centre
224 Banff Avenue
Banff, Canada
Telephone: (+1) 403 762 1550
www.pc.gc.ca/banff

Lake Louise Visitor Centre
Village of Lake Louise, next to the Samson Mall
Telephone: (+1) 403 522 3833

Kootenay Information Centre
Radium Hot Springs
Telephone: (+1) 250 347 9615
www.pc.gc.ca/kootenay

Icefield Information Centre
At the Icefield Parkway (Athabasca Glacier)
Telephone: (+1) 780 852 6288

Jasper Visitor Centre
500 Connaught Drive (main street Jasper)
Jasper
Telephone: (+1) 780 852 6176
www.pc.gc.ca/jasper

Mount Robson Visitor Centre
Highway 16
Mount Robson, British Columbia
Telephone: (+1) 800 435 5622
www.bcparks.ca

Maps

We have included descriptive waypoints and maps to help you find your way. The waypoints should give you brief and, as much as possible, accurate information on the major decision point during your hike.

However, please note that the maps are intended for general orientation only and therefore exact details are not guaranteed. The most reliable maps, in our opinion, are the Gem Trek Maps. Each hike description includes a Gem Trek map reference. These maps do not include elaborate trail details but they do show a larger landscape area thus ensuring easier orientation and accurate identification of sights and locations (surrounding peaks, etc). The Gem Trek Maps can be purchased at the Parks Canada kiosks.

Compass bearings

In the Canadian Rockies, the compass deviation is approximately 19 degrees west so true north lies 19 degrees west of the magnetic north.

Be bear safe and well-equipped

Before starting your hike, ensure that you have all the necessary hiking equipment, appropriate clothing and a sufficient amount of food and water. It is also of utmost importance that you hike "bear safe" by equipping yourself with a sufficient level of knowledge on how to behave when you see a bear. Study the "Guide to Safety and Conservation on the Trail" on the Parks Canada website: http://www.pc.gc.ca.

Always check at Parks Canada visitor centres for the latest information so that you can take the right precautions. Most notably, bring a bear bell, bear spray and make noise as you walk; keep children close to you and watch out for bear signs along your way such as fresh bear droppings (a clear signal of bear activity within close vicinity). Always keep your distance from any wild animal.

Don't leave anything behind

Please make every effort to ensure the Canadian Rockies remain beautiful. Never leave any food or traces behind such as soiled toilet paper and be sure to carry plastic bags for transporting your personal waste.

Stay on the trails

Stick to the established trails. It is dangerous and potentially damaging to the natural environment to stray from the path.

Weather

In the mountains, the weather can change without warning so you should always be prepared for adverse weather conditions. Take plenty of warm clothes as temperatures fluctuate rapidly.

When you hike in the mountains and above the tree line, you are exposed to the risk of thunderstorms and lightning. It is essential that you are aware of the weather forecast before embarking on your hike.

Bear habitat & group access

There are a few areas where Parks Canada restricts hiking on trails to protect bear habitat, especially around Lake Louise and Moraine Lake. Hiking regulations may insist that you hike in groups of at least four. It is advisable to check with the local Visitor Centre for current regulations before setting out on your hike. You can also find accurate and reliable information on the Parks Canada website.

Bus to the Lake O'Hara area

Parks Canada has limited the number of seats on the public bus service into Lake O'Hara to ensure ecological preservation of this highly popular area. The daily quota is 42 users (as of 2009, but note this information may change from year to year). To take the bus to Lake O'Hara, you need to make reservations well in advance (relevant fees apply). The bus operates from mid-June until the first weekend in October (start and end dates may vary from year to year). The bus departs from a sign-posted parking lot 15 km east of Field. Buses for day visitors depart between mid-June and early October at 8:30 a.m. and 10:30 a.m. returning at 3:30 p.m. and 6:30 p.m.

You are entitled to make reservations up to three calendar months in advance. Reservations can only be made by calling (+1) 250 343 6433 at a cost of $15 / person (2009) plus $12 reservation/booking fee. For the latest information, see the Yoho National Park pages on the Parks Canada website (www.pc.ga.ca/yoho) or go to the Visitor Centre in Field. In addition, every day, six seats are allocated for the following day on a first-come, first-served basis at the Field Visitor Centre. The centre officially opens at 9 a.m. but it is best to arrive early as there is usually no shortage of visitors interested in these remaining seats.

If you are interested to visit the O'Hara area but don't have a reservation, note that it is possible to walk to Lake O'Hara (11 km one way) from the Trans-Canada Highway. Normally it is no problem taking the outbound bus leaving from O'Hara Lake at the end of the day ($9.75/person). A reservation for this service is not required (2009).

Note regarding Geraldine Lakes (Jasper)

Owing to the great difficulty in following this beautiful trail we did not include it in the top list. To hike here you will need advanced route-finding skills.

List of presented hikes

Yoho area

Hike Nr.	Page Nr.	Hike Name	Round-Trip Distance (km)	Elevation Gain (m)	Duration (hrs)	Difficulty: Very Easy (1) - Strenuous (5)
1	18	Lake O'Hara & Lake Oesa Circuit	7.3	240	3 - 4	2 - Easy
2	21	Lake McArthur	7	305	3 - 4	2 - Easy
3	24	Wiwaxy Gap & Opabin Lake Circuit	11.5	550	5 - 6	4 - Challenging
4	28	Emerald Lake Circuit	5.3	None	1.5	1 - Very Easy
5	31	Iceline - Complete Loop	21.6	750	7 - 8	5 - Strenuous
5	31	Iceline - Shortcut via Celeste Lake	17.6	600	5 - 6	5 - Strenuous
5	31	Iceline Summit	14.5	700	4 - 5	5 - Strenuous
6	36	Twin Falls & Whaleback Circuit	21.6	690	7 - 8	5 - Strenuous
6	36	Twin Falls - Shortcut via Marpole Lake	17.3	300	5	3 - Moderate
7	42	Sherbrooke Lake	6 - 9	260	3 - 4	2 - Easy
7	42	Paget Lookout	6.8	530	4	3 - Moderate
7	42	Niles Meadows	17.6	650	6 - 8	4 - Challenging

List of presented hikes

Lake Louise & Moraine Lake area

Hike Nr.	Page Nr.	Hike Name	Round-Trip Distance (km)	Elevation Gain (m)	Duration (hrs)	Difficulty: Very Easy (1) - Strenuous (5)
8	46	Plain of the Six Glaciers	13.4	475	4 - 5	3 - Moderate
9	49	Larch Valley to Sentinel Pass	11.8	750	4 - 5	4 - Challenging
10	53	Eiffel Lake	11.2	380	3 - 4	3 - Moderate
10	53	Wenkchemna Pass	19.5	720	6 - 7	5 - Strenuous
11	57	Fairview Mountain & Saddleback Pass	10.4	610	4 - 5	4 - Challenging
12	61	Paradise Valley trail to Annette Lake	11.4	245	3 - 4	2 - Easy
13	64	Taylor Lake & O'Brien Lake	12.4	600	5 - 6	3 - Moderate

List of presented hikes

North Kootenay & Banff area

Hike Nr.	Page Nr.	Hike Name	Round-Trip Distance (km)	Elevation Gain (m)	Duration (hrs)	Difficulty: Very Easy (1) - Strenuous (5)
14	67	Stanley Glacier	9.6	350	3	3 - Moderate
15	69	Johnston Canyon	5.6	130	1 - 2	1 - Very Easy
15	69	Johnston Canyon & Inkpots	12	325	3 - 4	3 - Moderate
16	73	Bourgeau Lake	15	710	5	4 - Challenging
16	73	Mount Bourgeau	24	1490	8	5 - Strenuous
17	78	Cory Pass - Mount Edith Loop	13.2	910	6	5 - Strenuous
18	82	C-Level Cirque	8.4	465	3 - 4	3 - Moderate
19	85	Lake Minnewanka	15	40	3 - 4	2 - Easy

List of presented hikes

Bow Lake & Columbia Icefield area

Hike Nr.	Page Nr.	Hike Name	Round-Trip Distance (km)	Elevation Gain (m)	Duration (hrs)	Difficulty: Very Easy (1) - Strenuous (5)
20	88	Helen Lake	12	425	4 - 5	3 - Moderate
20	88	Katherine Lake	16.2	675	5 - 6	3 - Moderate
21	92	Bow Glacier Falls	9.2	145	3	2 - Easy
22	96	Bow Summit Lookout	6.2	230	2	2 - Easy
23	99	Caldron Lake	15.6	905	7 - 8	5 - Strenuous
24	103	Nigel Pass	14.4	365	4 - 5	3 - Moderate
25	107	Parker Ridge	5.6	250	2	2 - Easy
26	110	Wilcox Pass	8	355	3	3 - Moderate

List of presented hikes

Jasper & Mount Robson area

Hike Nr.	Page Nr.	Hike Name	Round-Trip Distance (km)	Elevation Gain (m)	Duration (hrs)	Difficulty: Very Easy (1) - Strenuous (5)
27	113	Cavell Meadows	8	520	2 - 3	3 - Moderate
28	117	Bald Hills	13.4	630	4 - 5	4 - Challenging
29	121	Opal Hills	8.2	460	3 - 4	4 - Challenging
30	124	Jacques Lake	23	90	6 - 7	3 - Moderate
30	124	Jacques Lake trail to Second Summit Lake	12	90	3 - 4	2 - Easy
31	128	Maligne Canyon	8.8	110	2 - 3	1 - Very Easy
32	131	Sulphur Skyline	9.6	690	3 - 4	4 - Challenging
33	133	Berg Lake trail to Kinney Lake	10	130	3	2 - Easy

1   Lake O'Hara & Lake Oesa Circuit

ROUND-TRIP DISTANCE:	7.3 km
TIME NEEDED:	3 - 4 hrs
ELEVATION GAIN:	240 m
LEVEL:	Easy
PERIOD:	early July - end of September
GEM TREK MAP:	Lake Louise & Yoho

The Lake O'Hara area is one of the most spectacular places in Canada. This area has simply some of the most breathtaking scenery in the Canadian Rockies. The Lake O'Hara & Lake Oesa Circuit is a combination of two short trails (the Lake O'Hara lakeshore trail and the Lake Oesa trail) passing several alpine lakes, mountain peaks, a waterfall and wildflower covered meadows. Anyone planning to hike here can look forward to a straightforward yet marvellous hike in a breathtaking scenic landscape.

Please note that Parks Canada has limited the number of visitors per day in the Lake O'Hara area and that group access restrictions may apply. For further information, see pages 10 and 11.

Waypoints

1. The lakeshore trailhead (elevation level of 2035 m) is located in the north-west corner of Lake O'Hara, about 100 metres north of the Warden Cabin and the Relais Hut. From the trailhead walk in a north-easterly direction.
2. 0.1 km - You cross the Cataract Brook Bridge.
3. 0.2 km - You arrive at the junction with the Wiwaxy Gap trail (trail to your left). Ignore this trail to the Wiwaxy Gap, go straight (right) and follow the beautiful shoreline (east).
4. 0.9 km - You arrive at the junction with the Lake Oesa trail (trail to your left). Go left here. The trail starts ascending (with switchbacks) on a steep cliff.
5. 2.5 km - You arrive at the junction with Yukness Ledge Alpine Route (trail to your right). Ignore this trail. Continue on the Lake Oesa trail.
6. 2.6 km - You arrive at Victoria Lake.
7. 3.0 km - You arrive at the junction with the Wiwaxy Gap trail (left). Continue on the Lake Oesa trail.
8. 3.2 km - You arrive at Lake Oesa. From here, take the same route back on the Lake Oesa trail.
9. 5.5 km - You arrive at the junction of the Lake Oesa trail and the O'Hara lakeshore trail. Go left on the O'Hara lakeshore trail.
10. 5.8 km - You pass the Seven Veils Falls, a beautiful viewpoint to enjoy for a while.
11. 6.1 km - As you continue along the lakeshore, you pass (see map) a junction with the East Opabin trail to your left. Go straight on the Lakeshore trail.
12. 6.8 km - You arrive at the junction where the trail on your left leads to the Opabin Plateau and Mary Lake. Both are really worthwhile and you may decide to continue on these loops. See also hike 3, Wiwaxy Gap - Opabin Lake Circuit for more information.
13. 7.3 km - You arrive back at the Warden Cabin.

Driving directions

For directions to the Lake O'Hara area see pages 10 and 11.

Lake O'Hara & Lake Oesa Circuit

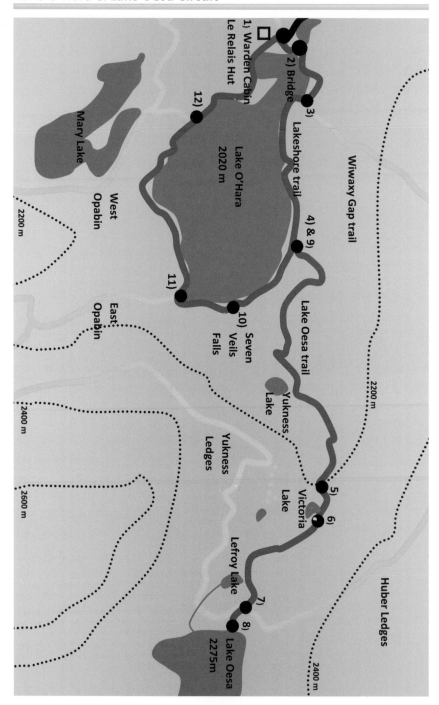

2   Lake McArthur

ROUND-TRIP DISTANCE: 7.0 km
TIME NEEDED: 3 - 4 hrs
ELEVATION GAIN: 305 m
LEVEL: Easy
PERIOD: early July - end of September
GEM TREK MAP: Lake Louise & Yoho

A wonderful hike! This is a short hike on a very beautiful alpine trail. Due to the diversity of the scenery, you may forget that this trail does have some elevation gain. So before you know, you arrive at Lake McArthur – the largest lake in the O'Hara region.

Please note that Parks Canada has limited the number of visitors per day in the Lake O'Hara area and that group access restrictions may apply. For further information, see pages 10 and 11.

Waypoints

1. The trail starts at the Relais Hut (2035 m). From here, you walk 300 metres southwest (see map).
2. 0.3 km - You arrive at a junction. The trail to your left leads to Big Larches and the Mary Lake Loop. Take the McArthur Pass trail. This is the trail on your right. You enter an open alpine meadow land.
3. 0.6 km - You arrive at the junction with the Linda Lake Circuit (to your right). Continue (left) on the McArthur Pass. You pass the Elisabeth Parker Hut and then you enter the forested area again.

The trail continues its gentle ascent.

4. 1.5 km - You pass the junction with the Big Larches trail (left). Continue to Schaffer Lake. Cross the bridge to the other side of the creek.

5. 1.6 km - You arrive at a junction on the south side of Schaffer Lake. The trail on the right is the McArthur Pass trail. The trail on the left is the McArthur High trail. Take the McArthur High trail that follows the shoreline of the Schaffer Lake.

6. 2.4 km - You arrive at a junction. Continue on the McArthur High trail (go left). You continue to climb for another 0.5 km until you reach the highest point of the trail (2340 metres).

7. 3.5 km - You arrive at Lake McArthur. Enjoy the deep blue lake and the unforgettable panorama. From here you can take the same way back or take the McArthur Low trail (from Lake McArthur the trail is going in a north-easterly direction).

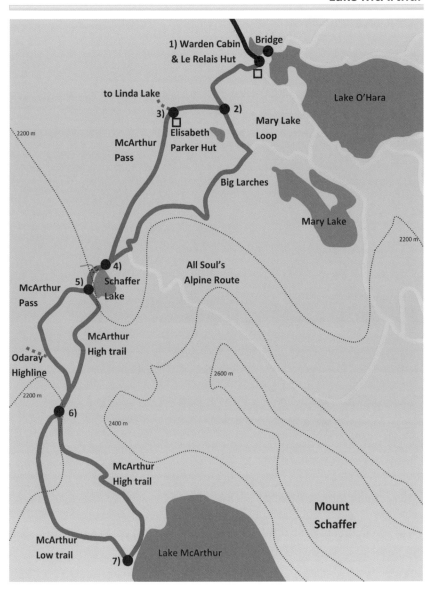

Driving directions

For directions to the Lake O'Hara area see pages 10 and 11.

3   Wiwaxy Gap & Opabin Lake Circuit

ROUND-TRIP DISTANCE:	11.5 km
TIME NEEDED:	5 - 6 hrs
ELEVATION GAIN:	550 m
LEVEL:	Challenging
PERIOD:	end July - end of September
GEM TREK MAP:	Lake Louise & Yoho

This hike is really stunningly beautiful and simply one of the most overwhelmingly engaging hikes in the Canadian Rockies, but you should be fit and prepared. It is a very steep trail up and down the Wiwaxy Gap. The first part of this hike takes you up from 2035 metres to 2530 metres in the first 2 km. The views are spectacular on Wiwaxy Gap where you can absorb the most panoramic view of the Lake O'Hara region.

Be aware that at this height there is a risk that you may end up in the snow even in the middle of the summer, so do not forget to pack the appropriate clothing. Descending from Wiwaxy Gap can be somewhat difficult especially when the trail is wet or icy. It may also be a little unpleasant for people with fear of heights or lacking hiking experience on steep ridges.

In case of doubts, you are probably better off skipping this part of the Wiwaxy Gap & Opabin Lake Circuit. Instead, use waypoints 1-8 of hike 1 (Lake O'Hara & Lake Oesa Circuit) to get to Lake Oesa. From there continue at waypoint 4 of this hike. The second part of the trail from Lake Oesa down to Opabin Lake is not as strenuous as the first part though it continues to provide a very beautiful scenic experience. At Opabin Lake you have a good chance to see small wild life such as pikas, marmots and squirrels. You will likely see quite a few mountain goats on your way.

Please note that Parks Canada has limited the number of visitors per day in the Lake O'Hara area and that group access restrictions may apply. For further information, see pages 10 and 11.

Waypoints

1. The trailhead (elevation level of 2035 m) is located in the northwest corner of Lake O'Hara, just north of the Warden Cabin and the Relais Hut. From the trailhead walk north and cross the Cataract Brook bridge.
2. 0.2 km - You arrive at a junction with the trail to Wiwaxy Gap (left). Go left here. The trail will ascend steeply for the next 1.6 km. Soon you emerge above the tree line.
3. 2.1 km - You reach Wiwaxy Gap at an elevation level of 2530 metres. Enjoy stunning views over the valley. From here, the trail descends as you follow the Huber Ledges route (east). Pay attention as you go down and take it easy as some descents are surprisingly steep.
4. 4.1 km - You arrive at a junction with the Lake Oesa trail. Follow the Oesa Lake trail towards the lake and continue on the Yukness ledges trail (southerly direction). Cross the small stream as the trail curves west. You pass Lefroy Lake (on your right). The trail curves quickly north and then you continue towards Opabin Lake in a southerly direction.
5. 6.6 km - You arrive at a junction with the East Opabin trail. Go left here on the East Opabin trail to Opabin Lake.
6. 7.0 km - You arrive at Opabin Lake. From here, take the West Opabin trail (starting in a south-westerly direction and soon curving into a north-westerly direction).

7. 8.3 km - You arrive at a junction. The trail on your right goes to Hungabee Lake. Ignore this trail (or go right to take a look at the Lake). Continue (left trail, heading in a north-westerly direction) and cross a creek.

8. 9.0 km - You arrive at another junction. If you go straight, this trail will take you back to Lake O'Hara (north of the East Opabin trail). Go left here and cross a creek. To arrive at the Opabin Prospect turn right directly after the creek, or if you decide to forego on the views from the Opabin Prospect, you can continue on the main trail. This saves you about 0.7 km hiking distance and some strenuous climbing up. If this is your decision, continue reading at waypoint 10.

9. 9.7 km - You arrive at Opabin Prospect, a marvellous viewpoint overlooking Mary Lake and Lake O'Hara. From here the trail curves south again, back to the main trail (West Opabin trail).

10. 10.1 km - You are back at the West Opabin trail (junction). Go right (north-westerly direction) towards Mary Lake.

11. 10.3 km - You reach a junction with the All Soul's Alpine Route to your left. Ignore this trail. Continue northwest on the West Opabin trail as you descend to Mary Lake.

12. 10.8 km - When passing the north shoreline of Mary Lake, you arrive at a junction with a trail leading to Lake O'Hara shoreline. Go right here.

13. 11.0 km - Take a left turn at the next junction on the Lake O'Hara shoreline loop.

14. 11.5 km - You return at the warden cabin on the west side of the O'Hara Lake.

Driving directions

For directions to the Lake O'Hara area see pages 10 and 11.

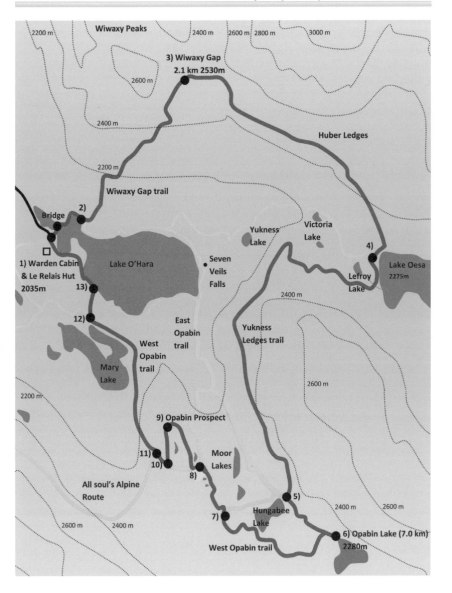

Wiwaxy Peaks

2200 m   2400 m   2600 m 2800 m   3000 m

3) Wiwaxy Gap
2.1 km 2530m

2600 m

Huber Ledges

2400 m

2200 m

Wiwaxy Gap trail

Bridge 2)

Yukness   Victoria
Lake   Lake

4)

1) Warden Cabin   Lake O'Hara
& Le Relais Hut   Seven
2035m   Veils
13)   Falls

Lake Oesa
2275m

Lefroy
Lake

2400 m

12)   East
                   Opabin   Yukness
West   trail   Ledges trail
Opabin
Mary   trail
Lake   2600 m

2200 m

9) Opabin Prospect

11)   Moor
10)   Lakes
           8)

All soul's Alpine
Route   5)

2400 m   2600 m

7)   Hungabee
           Lake

2600 m   2400 m   6) Opabin Lake (7.0 km)
                                            2280m
West Opabin trail

4   Emerald Lake Circuit

ROUND-TRIP DISTANCE: 5.3 km
TIME NEEDED: 1.5 hrs
ELEVATION GAIN: Negligible
LEVEL: Very Easy
PERIOD: June - October
GEM TREK MAP: Lake Louise & Yoho

Emerald Lake is one of the great natural treasures of Yoho National Park. The lake is truly beautiful – complemented by the stunning surrounding mountains and glaciers (including Emerald Glacier) and blessed with a large variety of flowers, birds and forested vegetation. It also offers a cornucopia of wildlife like ospreys, bald eagles and moose. The Emerald Lake Circuit is a beautiful walk and the easiest hike presented in this book. It is ideal for young and old and suitable for an early morning or evening walk, or just as a less physically demanding intermediate hike. Note, that usually it can be rather busy at Emerald Lake. On offer at the Lake, close to main parking and the bridge, is a bar/restaurant, where you can enjoy a drink and/or meal with a great view.

Waypoints

1. From the parking area, walk north along the shore. Don't cross the bridge. Walk clockwise around the lake on the paved trail (pavement ends after 300 metres).

2. 1.6 km - You arrive at a junction with the trail to Emerald Basin (left). Go straight (right trail). You are now on the north side of the Emerald Lake and from here you continue in an easterly direction.

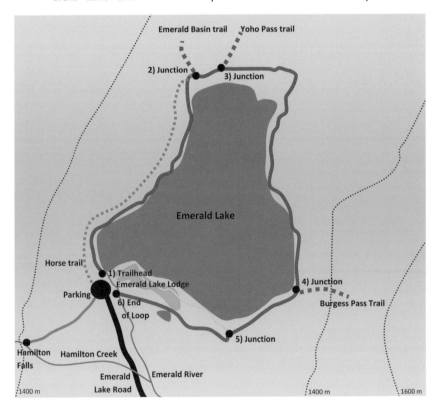

3. 1.7 km - You arrive at a junction with the Yoho Pass trail (left). Go straight (right trail). Continue on the lakeshore (easterly direction). Soon, you cross a small bridge (2.1 km).

4. 3.8 km - You arrive at a junction with Burgess Pass trail (left). Continue on the lakeshore trail gradually curving west.

5. 4.7 km - You arrive at the parking area of the Emerald Lake Lodge complex. Go left here towards the Peaceful Pond. After 300 metres, turn left

again at the junction behind the Emerald Lake lodge building or you can take the small trail just behind the Emerald Lake Lodge parking area.

6. 5.3 km - You return at the parking area.

A family from Vancouver on a hike at Emerald Lake

Driving directions

From the Trans-Canada Highway take the Emerald Lake Road (1.5 km west of Field). The trailhead is on the northside of the parking lot, beside the bridge.

5   Iceline

ROUND-TRIP DISTANCE:	21.6 km for the complete Iceline loop
	17.6 km for Shortcut via Celeste Lake
	14.5 km for Iceline Summit
TIME NEEDED:	Iceline: 7 - 8 hrs
	Shortcut route: 5 - 6 hrs
	Iceline summit: 4 - 5 hrs
ELEVATION GAIN:	Iceline: 750 m
	Shortcut route: 600 m
	Iceline summit: 700 m
LEVEL:	Strenuous (all)
PERIOD:	mid July - end of September
GEM TREK MAP:	Lake Louise & Yoho

The Iceline is Yoho's most popular longer day hike. This hike has wonderful scenery in a landscape covered by glaciers as recently as 100 years ago. It is a must for every fit hiker visiting Yoho. The Iceline is a magnificent hike, but also long and quite arduous with a total distance of 21 km and 700 metres of elevation gain to the summit. From the summit you will experience some beautiful views of a major part of the amazing Yoho Valley including Emerald Glacier.

Iceline

A shorter route to consider is a hike to the Iceline Summit (point 5 in the map) returning back the same way (6.7 km one way, 13.4 km return). Another alternative route is a shorter 17.6 km loop passing Celeste Lake. To take the shortcut route you follow after 5.8 km (waypoint 4, see map) the Celeste Lake trail for 4.2 km until you reach the Little Yoho Valley trail (waypoint 7 in the map).

Waypoints

From the parking area at Takakkaw Falls you walk south to the trailhead at the Whiskey Jack hostel (0.6 km).

1. The trail starts with a steady climb (with switchbacks) as you walk through a beautiful forested area. Starting at the Whiskey Jack Hostel at an elevation level of 1520 metres, you will go up to an elevation level of 2215 metres - the highest point on the trail - covering a distance of 6.7 km. En route you pass a forested area with limestone ridges and rocky slopes.

2. 1 km - You arrive at a junction with a path to Hidden Lakes (left). Continue on the Iceline trail. After 200 metres, you reach another junction. The trail to the left leads to Yoho Pass. Ignore this trail and continue on the Iceline trail.

3. 2.5 km - You arrive at a junction with the Yoho Lake trail (left). Ignore this trail and continue on the Iceline trail.

4. 5.8 km - You arrive at a junction with a trail to Celeste Lake and Twin Falls (right). Continue on the Iceline trail (left) or if you choose to go for the short 17.6 km alternative, go right here on the Celeste Lake trail. For the shortcut route via Celeste Lake you walk for 4.2 km (north) following the Celeste Lake trail. You pass Celeste Lake before you reach the Little Yoho Valley trail. From here, continue at waypoint 7.

5. 6.7 km - You reach the summit of the Iceline trail. A good moment to take a short break and to enjoy the panoramic views over the valley including Emerald glacier, the Isolation peak and the Waputik glacier Icefield. From here, the trail starts descending and soon you enter a forested alpine area.

6. 10.4 km - You arrive at the junction with a trail leading to the Kiwetinok Pass (left). Continue on the main trail (right). A little further, you will reach the Little Yoho River. To continue, keep right, cross the bridge (Little Yoho River Bridge) and go right. The Little Yoho Campground will

be to your left at this point. You are now on the Little Yoho Valley trail. You pass the Stanley Mitchell Hut.

7. 14.0 km - You pass a junction (right) with a trail to Celeste Lake. Keep straight. If you have chosen the shortcut route at waypoint 4, this is where you get back on the Iceline route (from the Little Yoho Valley trail).

8. 14.1 km - You arrive at another junction. The Whaleback trail is to your left. Continue straight.

9. 14.6 km - You arrive at a junction. The Marpole Connector trail to your left leads to the Twin Falls (3.3 km north). Continue on the Little Yoho Valley trail.

10. 16.2 km - You arrive at a junction at Laughing Falls. At this point the Little Yoho Valley trail and the Yoho Valley trail meet. Continue on the Yoho Valley trail. Take a right turn here (south), towards Takakkaw Falls. You soon pass a junction with a short path towards the Duchesnay Lake. Note: Duchesnay Lake may be much smaller than it looks on the map as it dries up during the summer season.

11. 18.5 km - You arrive at the junction of Lace Falls and Angel's staircase viewpoint. It is only a short walk to these worthwhile falls. The Lace Falls are to your right and Angel's staircase to your left.

12. 21 km - You return to the Takakkaw Falls parking lot.

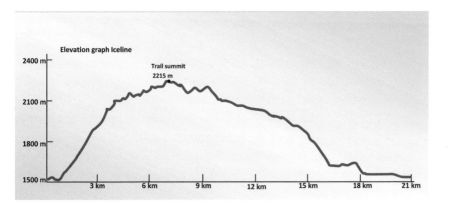

Iceline

Takakkaw Falls

Driving directions

From the Trans-Canada Highway take the Yoho Valley Road (East of Field). You can park at the parking lot of the Takakkaw Falls. It is a 600 metres walk to the Whiskey Jack Hostel where the trailhead is located (see map).

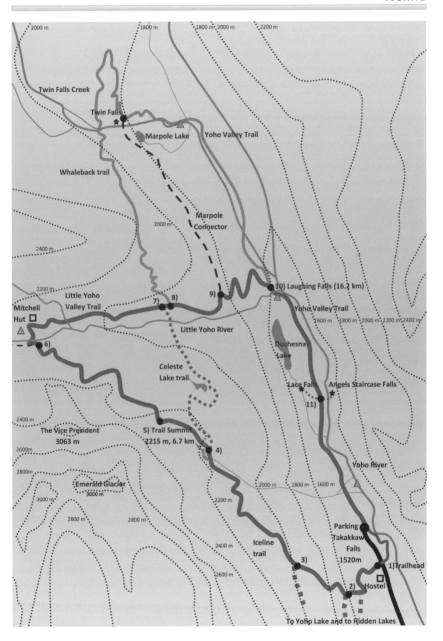

6   Twin Falls & Whaleback Circuit

ROUND-TRIP DISTANCE: 21.6 km for Twin Falls & Whaleback Circuit
17.3 km shortcut via Marpole Lake

TIME NEEDED: Twin Falls & Whaleback Circuit: 7 - 8 hrs
Shortcut route: 5 hrs

ELEVATION GAIN: Twin Falls & Whaleback Circuit: 690 m
Shortcut route: 300 m

LEVEL: Twin Falls & Whaleback Circuit: Strenuous
Shortcut route: Moderate

PERIOD: mid July - end of September
GEM TREK MAP: Lake Louise & Yoho

Twin Falls - Whaleback is another brilliant hike in the Yoho Valley. Just like the Iceline (day hike 5 in this book), this hike is long and strenuous, but absolutely worth it. If you are drawn to impressive waterfalls and the most superb valley views, then this hike should be your choice for the day. You will pass a total of 5 waterfalls including the Takakkaw waterfalls at the start of the hike.

What makes this hike really special is the marvellous diversity in scenery during the loop. At the summit of the Whaleback trail you will have superb views covering a significant area of Yoho Valley and the surrounding mountain peaks and glaciers.

Laughing Falls

An easier alternative returning route:
You may like to see the Twin Falls but are not looking for a strenuous climb to the summit of the Whaleback trail. Then, follow from the Twin Falls junction (way-point 6 in the map) the Marpole Connector (in southerly direction). From there, back to the junction with the Little Yoho Valley trail (waypoint 10 in the map).

A more strenuous, longer returning route:
If you are in excellent condition, have sufficient time (start early) and you are willing to hike an additional 7 km (28 km in total), then you could combine the best of the Iceline route with this route. When you arrive at the end of the Whaleback trail (point 9, 14.8 km), you turn right (instead of turning left) and continue on the Little Yoho Valley trail (follow the Iceline description, day hike 5, in the opposite walking direction). It is a superb addition to the route, but you will need a full day to complete it. Moreover, you should be really fit to make the most of it and to derive full enjoyment as it is the most arduous hike.

Twin Falls & Whaleback Circuit

Waypoints

1. You will find the Yoho Valley trailhead on the north side of the Takakkaw Falls parking area. The trail starts on a wide road (heading north) and follows the Yoho River upstream (Yoho River is to your right). After 350 metres you pass the Takakkaw Falls campground.

2. 2.2 km - You reach the junction with the Angels Staircase viewpoint on your right and Pont Lace Falls on your left. Both falls are well worth visiting. Continuing on the main trail, you pass Duchesnay Lake which may be a great deal smaller than it appears on the map as it dries up during the summer. Continue on the main trail (Yoho Valley trail, heading in a northerly direction).

3. 4.4 km - You pass the Laughing Falls campground and Laughing Falls as you arrive at the junction with the Little Yoho Valley trail (left). Continue on the Yoho Valley trail (right, continue in a northerly direction) towards Twin Falls.

4. 4.8 km - You cross the Twin Falls Creek bridge.

5. 6.5 km - You arrive at a junction with the Yoho Glacier trail (right). Continue on the Yoho Valley trail (left) to Twin Falls. Cross the bridge over the Twin Falls Creek and pass the Twin Falls campground

(on your left). The trail starts ascending again (with switchbacks).

6. 8.2 km - You arrive at a junction at the Twin Falls Chalet. The trail to your left leads to the Twin Falls Chalet and the Marpole Connector trail. *For the shorter hiking route, you go left here via the Marpole Connector. Follow this trail going south to the Little Yoho Valley trail (waypoint 10).* The trail to your right is the Whaleback trail. Go right. It will not be long before you arrive at the base of the Twin Falls. From here, the trail starts ascending untill you reach the top of the Twin Falls (be careful not to go

near the steep rocky drop). From this elevated viewpoint on the cliff, you will descend again to the level of the Twin Falls Creek. Be careful on your way down as it is a rather steep descend.

7. 11 km - You arrive at the suspension bridge over the Twin Falls Creek. Cross the bridge. The road soon starts climbing to the summit of the Whaleback trail. It is a strenuous climb up.

8. 12.6 km - You reach the summit of the Whaleback trail at an elevation level of 2210 metres. Enjoy the view.

9. 14.8 km - You arrive at the junction with the Little Yoho Valley trail. Go left here in an easterly direction towards Laughing Falls.

10. 15.4 km - You arrive at a junction with the Marpole Lake Connector trail (left). Continue on the Little Yoho Valley trail to Laughing Falls.

11. 17.1 km - You arrive at the Laughing Falls junction. Turn left on the Yoho Valley trail towards Takakkaw Falls.

12. 21.6 km - You return to the Takakkaw Falls parking lot.

Driving directions

From the Trans-Canada Highway take the Yoho Valley Road (east of Field). You can park at the parking lot of the Takakkaw Falls.

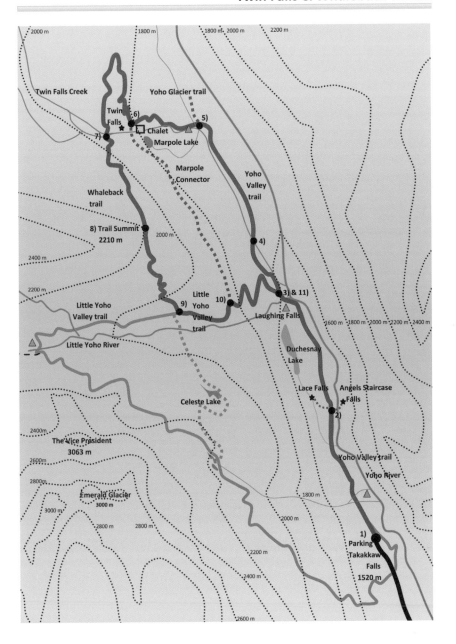

7   Sherbrooke Lake & Niles Meadows

ROUND-TRIP DISTANCE: Sherbrooke Lake: 6 - 9 km

Paget Lookout: 6.8 km

Niles Meadows: 17.6 km

TIME NEEDED: Sherbrooke Lake: 3 - 4 hrs

Paget Lookout: 4 hrs

Niles Meadows: 6 - 8 hrs

ELEVATION GAIN: Sherbrooke Lake: 260 m

Paget Lookout: 530 m

Niles Meadows: 650 m

LEVEL: Sherbrooke Lake: Easy

Paget Lookout: Moderate

Niles Meadows: Challenging

PERIOD: mid July - end of September

GEM TREK MAP: Lake Louise & Yoho

From the Wapta Lake parking area you can choose from three worthwhile hiking destinations: Sherbrooke Lake, Paget Lookout and Niles Meadows. Sherbrooke Lake is the perfect easy-going hike for all abilities. It is not too far and the turquoise lake is a destination of entrancing splendour.

Bow Glacier Falls
Round-trip 9.2 km   Easy
elev. 145 meters time 3 hrs

Helen Lake
Round-trip 12km   time 5 hrs
elev. 425 meters Moderate

Bow Summit Lookout
Round-trip 6.2 km   Easy
time 2 hrs elev. 230 meters

Nigel Pass
Round-trip 14.4 kms Moderate
elev. 365 meters time 5hrs
final 2 kms hardest to Pass

Wilcox Pass
round-trip 8 kms   Moderate
elev. 355 meters

Jasper

- Bald Hills, Opal Hills — Challenging
- M) Jacques Lake — Moderate (6-7hrs)
- J) Sulphur Skyline — Challenging

Columbia Icefield
- Nigel Pass — moderate (4-5hrs)
- Wilcox Pass — moderate
- Parker Ridge — easy

Banff
- Larch Valley, Sentinel Pass — Challenging

You will enjoy the nature at its best here and compared to Emerald Lake it is quiet – a sanctuary for those seeking solitude. A nice addition to the Sherbrooke Lake hike is the trail to Paget Lookout. It is a short but steady hike up (2 km from the junction with the Sherbrooke Lake trail). On the lookout, a former fire lookout post, you can enjoy excellent views over Lake O'Hara, the Kicking Horse Pass and Bow Valley.

The most rewarding part however is the trail from Sherbrooke Lake to Niles Meadows. The trail continues from the north side of Sherbrooke Lake. It can be a very muddy trail from time to time, which makes this hike a lot more strenuous. The trail follows the Sherbrooke Creek and passes a few beautiful waterfalls. After little more than a kilometre from the north shore of Sherbrooke Lake you arrive in the first beautiful meadow, a more accommodating place for a picnic than Sherbrooke Lake. From here, it is another 3 km to Niles Meadows - a pleasant trail and great fun to walk. The giant peaks of Niles Meadows will offer you great views in all directions like Cathedral Mountain and the peaks of the Lake O'Hara area to the south, Mount Ogden to the west, Mount Daly to the north and Paget Peak to the east.

Waypoints

1. The trailhead is at the far north end of the picnic area, just beyond the sheltered picnic area. The trail starts on a very clear path in a northerly direction. You soon arrive at the first junction. The path to the right is to the West Louise Lodge. Turn left here. The trail starts ascending through dense forest.
2. 1.4 km - You pass a junction with the trail to the Paget Lookout (to your right). When you are in for a great viewpoint you take a right turn here and go to the Paget Lookout. For Sherbrooke Lake and Niles Meadows, you continue on the main trail. The trail continues with a gentle ascent until it gradually levels out towards the basin of Sherbrooke Lake (2 km).
3. 3 km - You arrive at the south corner of Sherbrooke Lake. The trail continues along the east side of the lake towards Niles Meadows. As you continue walking north, you soon arrive at a small path to the left where you can walk to the lakeshore.

Sherbrooke Lake & Niles Meadows

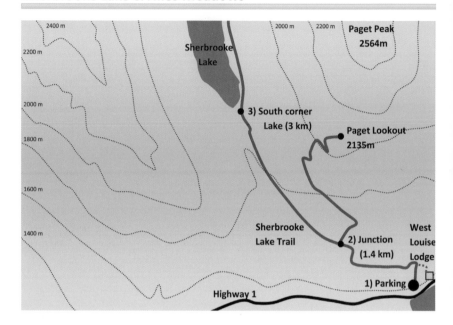

4. 4.4 km - You arrive at the north side of the Sherbrooke Lake (see second map for this hike on the next page). From here, you can continue for another 4.4 km to Niles Meadows (north) where the views are breathtaking. On your way, you also pass a few beautiful waterfalls. From this point on, the trail does not appear to be maintained. You first enter a forest which is then followed by an uphill trail. You will soon pass the first cascade.

5. 5.7 km - The views open up when you reach the beautiful meadows - an ideal place for a picnic.

6. 5.9 km - You cross a small footbridge over the streams in the meadows.

7. 6.1 km - You cross the bridge over the Niles Creek. From here, the trail continues again in a forested area. Soon, you pass another waterfall (around 7 km).

8. 7.6 km - You cross the Sherbrooke Creek (old log bridge).

9. 8.0 km - You cross the Sherbrooke Creek again (a functioning bridge but old and damaged). You soon pass (on your left) another waterfall.

10. 8.8 km - You enter Niles Meadows. Enjoy the great views before taking the same route back or you can continue going uphill on one of the higher ridges towards Mount Niles. The scenery on offer makes this an attractive option if feeling inclined, but be warned it soon becomes more of a scramble than a hike.

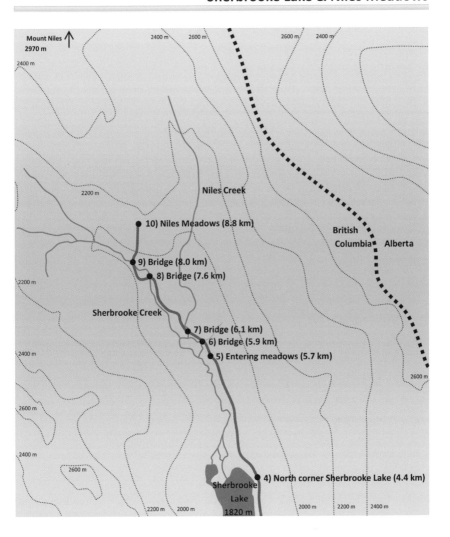

Mount Niles 2970 m
2400 m
2400 m 2600 m 2600 m 2400 m

Niles Creek

2200 m

10) Niles Meadows (8.8 km)

British Columbia Alberta

9) Bridge (8.0 km)
8) Bridge (7.6 km)
2200 m

Sherbrooke Creek

7) Bridge (6.1 km)
6) Bridge (5.9 km)
2400 m 5) Entering meadows (5.7 km)

2600 m

2600 m

2400 m

2600 m

4) North corner Sherbrooke Lake (4.4 km)

Sherbrooke Lake 1820 m

2200 m 2000 m 2000 m 2200 m 2400 m

Driving Directions

The Wapta Lake picnic area is located 11 km east of Field on Highway 1 (Trans-Canada Highway). You find the (unsigned) parking area on the north side of the road.

8   Plain of the Six Glaciers

ROUND-TRIP DISTANCE:	13.4 km
TIME NEEDED:	4 - 5 hrs
ELEVATION GAIN:	335 m to the teahouse, 475 m to viewpoint
LEVEL:	Moderate
PERIOD:	mid June - early October
GEM TREK MAP:	Lake Louise & Yoho

The Plain of Six Glaciers trail is a very popular hike, starting at one of the most photographed lakes of the Canadian Rockies. The trail takes you up to the foot of Mount Victoria's east face. Going up, you will pass avalanche slopes and glacial moraines, finally reaching the crest of a narrow lateral moraine with magnificent views of Mount Lefroy, Abbot Pass, Mount Victoria and of course Lake Louise.

On your way, you may take a break at the teahouse up in the mountain, where you can enjoy a hot drink. Quite a few people visit this trail to the teahouse during the summer season. But even on a busy day it is still worth it. And if you start early in the morning you will avoid most of the crowds.

Waypoints

1. The hike starts in front of the Chateau Lake Louise, where you have probably the most photographed view in Banff - the beautiful Lake Louise with the rising mountains in the background. It may be really busy here, but most visitors don't go farther than the southwest tip of the Lake. Follow the trail along the lake. At the end of the lake, the trail continues with a modest ascent. The trail is clearly marked and easy to follow.

2. 3.4 km - You arrive at a junction with the Beehive trail (to your right). The Beehive trail is a short trail (see map) that leads to two small mountain lakes (Lake Agnes & Mirror Lake) with some wonderfully elevated viewpoints. Continue on the Plain of the Six Glaciers trail (go straight).
3. 4.0 km - You pass another junction (to your right) also leading to Lake Agnes & Mirror Lake. Continue straight.
4. 5.5 km - You have reached the Six Glaciers teahouse (2060 metres). A great place for a break and an enjoyable cup of tea or coffee. From here, continue walking up to an even more elevated and superior viewpoint. From the teahouse, the trail continues for approximately 1.2 km with another elevation gain of 140 metres.

Plain of the Six Glaciers

5. 6.7 km - You arrive at the highest viewpoint of this trail at an elevation level of approximately 2200 metres. Enjoy the view on Mount Victoria, Victoria Glacier and Lake Louise. From here, take the same route back. If you feel strong enough and would like to add another 1 - 1.5 hours of hiking on your way back, you may consider turning left at waypoint 3 (see map) towards the Beehive trail (Lake Agnes & Mirror Lake).

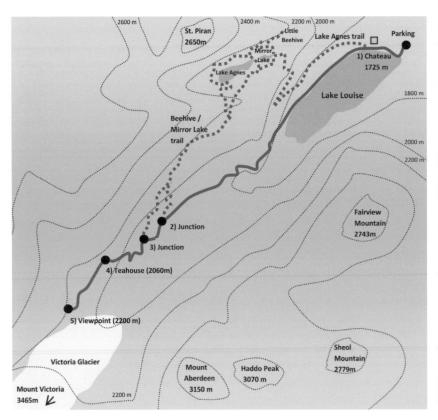

Driving directions

Follow the signs in Lake Louise Village towards the lake. You will arrive at the large parking lot. To get to the trailhead, walk to the lake and follow the lakeshore towards the Chateau.

9   Larch Valley to Sentinel Pass

ROUND-TRIP DISTANCE: 11.8 km
TIME NEEDED: 4 - 5 hrs
ELEVATION GAIN: 750 m
LEVEL: Challenging
PERIOD: mid July - end of September
GEM TREK MAP: Lake Louise & Yoho

Larch Valley to Sentinel Pass

The Larch Valley trail to Sentinel Pass is an absolutely wonderful hike. It is also a very popular hike in the Lake Louise and Moraine Lake area, considered by many the most beautiful area in Banff National Park. This hike starts at the beautiful Moraine Lake. From there you walk to Larch Valley, a great place to be especially in September when the larch trees change color and the valley is the most colourful of the year. On your way to Sentinel Pass, you will have the most fantastic panoramic and elevated views over Paradise Valley and on the Ten Peaks (the ten mountain peaks to the south of Moraine Lake). At the elevated viewpoints at Sentinel Pass you will be surrounded by mountain peaks with Pinnacle Mountain and Eiffel Peak to your left and Mount Temple to your right. It is a fantastic place.

Group access restrictions

The Moraine Lake area is an active grizzly bear habitat. Group access regulations may therefore be in effect. The reason for this regulation is to reduce the risk of bear confrontation. Group access regulations usually require you to hike in a tight group of four or more. A tight group means that the person in the front must be able to comfortably speak with the person at the back at all times. Ensure you are familiar with standard bear safety precautions (for e.g. bear spray is recommended). When all visitors are aware and comply with the bear-safe walking guidelines of Parks Canada, the risks are at an acceptable human safety level. Always check before you start on a hike at the Visitor Centre in Lake Louise on any bear activity in the area and the latest safety precautions (or areas that have been closed due to bear activity).

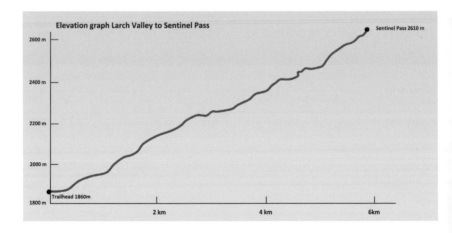

In case it is not possible to hike in the Moraine Lake area due to grizzly bear activity, possible alternatives are the hikes a little to the north around Lake Louise such as the Plain of the Six Glaciers (hike 8), Fairview Mountain (hike 11) or the less crowded Taylor Lake trail to the south (hike 13).

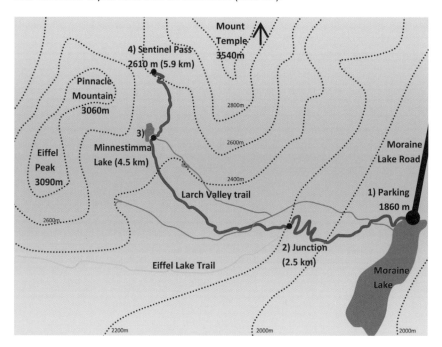

Waypoints

1. The Larch Valley trail starts at Moraine Lake (1860 metres). You will find the trailhead close to the lakeshore, just past the lodge (to your right). The hike starts with a moderate climb through a forest of Engelmann spruce and alpine fir.

2. 2.5 km - You arrive at a junction. Straight on will take you to the Eiffel Lake trail and Wenkchemna Pass. The trail to your right is the Larch Valley trail. Turn right here and continue along a gentle ascent. Soon, the views open up as you enter the wildflower meadows of Larch Valley (approximately 3.5 km). From here you will have a great view on the Valley of the Ten Peaks (south) and Mount Temple (northeast).

3. 4.5 km - You arrive at Minnestimma Lake. The trail continues with a steady ascent for the last 1.4 km towards Sentinel Pass.

4. 5.9 km - You arrive at the Sentinel Pass. Enjoy the stunning views on Pinnacle Mountain (southwest) and Eiffel Peak (southwest), Mount Temple (northeast) and the Ten Peaks (south). Return the way you came.

Driving directions

From Lake Louise village, take the Lake Louise Drive and turn left onto the Moraine Lake Road. The parking is at the end of the road towards the lake.

10   Eiffel Lake & Wenkchemna Pass

ROUND-TRIP DISTANCE: Eiffel Lake: 11.2 km
Wenkchemna Pass: 19.5 km

TIME NEEDED: Eiffel Lake: 3 - 4 hrs
Wenkchemna Pass: 6 - 7 hrs

ELEVATION GAIN: Eiffel Lake: 380 m
Wenkchemna Pass: 720 m

LEVEL: Eiffel Lake: Moderate
Wenkchemna Pass: Strenuous

PERIOD: mid July - end of September

GEM TREK MAP: Lake Louise & Yoho

The Eiffel Lake trail is another fabulous hike, just south of the Sentinel Pass also starting at the beautiful Moraine Lake. In fact, the first 2.5 km of the Sentinel Pass and Eiffel Lake trails are one and the same. Many people prefer the Sentinel Pass as it is somewhat more rewarding in terms of elevated views. However the Eiffel Lake trail is a very pleasant and less strenuous hike compared to Sentinel Pass with only 380 metres of elevation gain. The scenery on the Eiffel Lake trail is one of a kind. You will have fantastic views on Moraine Lake, the Wenkchemna glacier and the Ten Peaks (less elevated compared to Sentinel Pass but nearby).

Eiffel Lake & Wenkchemna Pass

The hike from Eiffel Lake to the Wenkchemna Pass is worthwhile but the weather should be clear to ensure you enjoy unrestricted views on the higher elevated part of the trail to the summit at Wenkchemna Pass.

Group access restrictions may apply (see information on group access, hike 9 Larch Valley to Sentinel Pass).

Six out of the Ten Peaks

Waypoints

1. The Eiffel Lake trail starts at the Moraine Lake (1860 metres). You find the trailhead near the lakeshore, just past the lodge (to your right). The hike starts with a moderate climb through a forest of Engelmann spruce and alpine fir.

2. 2.5 km - You arrive at the junction with the trail to Larch Valley and Sentinel Pass (to your right). Continue on the Eiffel Lake trail (go straight, west). From this point on, up to Eiffel Lake, the trail is a fairly easy walk as it is only going up and down gently. Soon, you emerge above the tree line entering open alpine slopes. The views open up on the Ten Peaks to the south (to your left) and Moraine Lake to the east.

3. 5.6 km - You reach an elevated viewpoint on a rocky ridge above Eiffel Lake. This is the end of the Eiffel Lake trail. It is better not to go down to the lake as it can be very slippery with loose stones and rocks.

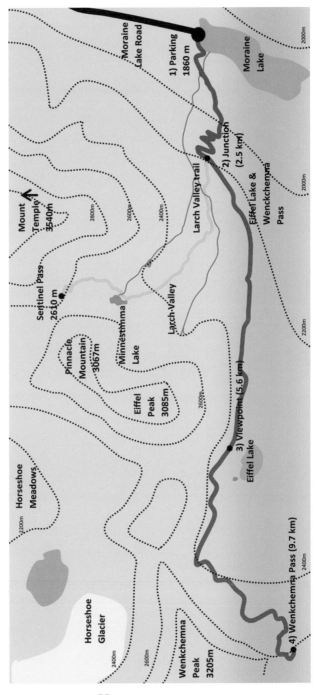

Eiffel Lake & Wenkchemna Pass

You can return the same way or continue to Wenkchemna Pass, which is an additional 4.1 km and 340 metres elevation gain. The trail steadily ascends (with switchbacks) over rocky alpine meadows. You cross a rocky moraine before you reach the foot of the Wenkchemna Peak. Then, the trail curves southwest over the lower level ridges of the Wenkchemna Peak.

4. 9.7 km - You reach the viewpoint at the summit of Wenkchemna Pass (2600 metres). Return the same way.

Driving directions

From Lake Louise village, take the Lake Louise Drive and turn left onto the Moraine Lake Road. The parking is at the end of the road towards the lake.

11   Fairview Mountain & Saddleback Pass

ROUND-TRIP DISTANCE: 10.4 km
TIME NEEDED: 4 - 5 hrs
ELEVATION GAIN: 610 m
LEVEL: Challenging
PERIOD: July - end of September
MAP: Lake Louise & Yoho

View on Victoria Glacier from Fairview Mountain

Fairview Mountain & Saddleback Pass

This trail leads you to the beautiful pass between Fairview Mountain and Saddleback Mountain where you will experience excellent views of the north face of Mount Temple and Paradise Valley. From Saddleback Pass (waypoint 4 on the map), you can continue to the highest accessible trail in the Banff National Park: the Fairview mountain summit with a height of 2743 metres. From there, you will have an unobstructed and beautiful view of the whole area at the most elevated viewpoint. The trail starts to the left of the popular viewpoint at Lake Louise and steadily climbs through forest and rocky slopes until you reach the magnificent alpine meadows. From here on, the trail just gets better all the way up. Important note: group access restrictions may apply for this hike (see information on group access, hike 9 Larch Valley to Sentinel Pass).

Lake Louise with the canoe rental (left)

Waypoints

1. You will find the trailhead at the north-eastern corner of the Lake, close to the boathouse/canoe rentals. The trail starts in a southerly direction.
2. 0.3 km - You arrive at a junction with the Fairview Lookout (right). Keep straight (south).

3. 0.4 km - You pass the junction with the Moraine Lake trail (left). Continue on the Saddleback trail (right). The trail starts ascending through dense forest and passes avalanche paths. Stay on the main trail to the left as it divides after approximately 1.5 km. The view soon opens up as you arrive into alpine meadows and fields of larches.

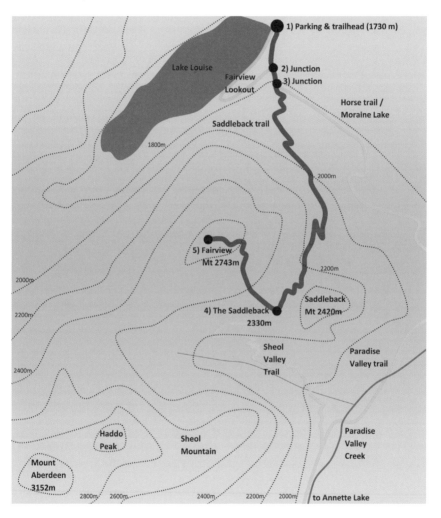

Fairview Mountain & Saddleback Pass

4. 3.7 km - As you reach the summit of the Saddleback Pass at an elevation of 2330 m, you arrive at the junction with the trail to Fairview Mountain (trail to your right). Straight ahead (veering left) is the trail to the Sheol Valley trail. Go right here to Fairview Mountain. From this point on, the trail is less clearly marked as you climb up some rocky slopes. There are many trail deviations caused by the intensive use of this trail over the years. Stay on the right course which heads in a north-westerly direction (see map). Be careful when rocks are wet.

5. 5.2 km - You arrive at the summit which has an amazing elevation level of 2743 metres. Enjoy the wonderful view. Take the same journey back.

Driving directions

Follow the signs in Lake Louise Village towards the lake. You will arrive at the large parking lot area. You are now on the east corner of the lake. You will find the trailhead at the viewpoint near the lake as you walk towards the boathouse/canoe rentals.

12   Paradise Valley trail to Annette Lake

ROUND-TRIP DISTANCE:	11.4 km
TIME NEEDED:	3 - 4 hours
ELEVATION GAIN:	245 m
LEVEL:	Easy - Moderate
PERIOD:	mid June - early October
MAP:	Lake Louise and Yoho

The Paradise Valley trail to Annette Lake is one of the easier hikes in the elevated Lake Louise and Moraine Lake area. This natural trail, just south of Lake Louise and north of Moraine Lake, perfectly guides you to the beautiful Annette Lake. The trail basically follows the Paradise Valley Creek with a total elevation gain of only 245 metres from trailhead up to Annette Lake.

To the north of the Valley, you pass some of the beguiling giant mountains like Fairview Mountain, Saddle Mountain, Sheol Mountain and Haddo Peak. To the south, you experience the majesty of Mount Temple with a height of 3544 metres. The view on the north face of Mount Temple from Annette Lake is impressive.

Paradise Valley trail to Annette Lake

Note: Group access restrictions may apply for this hike (see also information on group access at hike 9 Larch Valley to Sentinel Pass).

Waypoints

1. You find the trailhead (elevation level of 1720 metres) at the end of the parking area and start your hike on a well paved trail through a forest.
2. 1.0 km - You arrive at a junction with the Moraine Lake trail. Moraine Lake is to the left. Lake Louise is to the right. Go right for Paradise Valley & Annette Lake.
3. 1.2 km - You arrive at a junction with the Paradise Valley trail. Go left here.
4. 3.4 km - You arrive at the 1st bridge over the Paradise Valley Creek. From this point on the brilliant views of surrounding mountains open up. Continue on the east bank of the Paradise Valley Creek.
5. 3.9 km - You arrive at the 2nd bridge over the Paradise Valley Creek. Continue on the west bank of the Paradise Valley Creek.
6. 4.2 km - You arrive at a junction with the Sheol Valley trail (right) towards Fairview Mountain. Continue on the Paradise Valley trail (go straight).
7. 5.1 km - You arrive at the 3rd bridge over Paradise Valley Creek. Recross the creek once more and start the short walk over a steep rocky area to Annette Lake. Note that there is another small creek on your left as you walk in the direction of Annette Lake.
8. 5.7 km - You reach Annette Lake (elevation level of 1965 metres). Enjoy the overwhelming view of Annette Lake with the towering face of Mount Temple (south-east, 3544 metres). Take the same route back or continue from here for another kilometre to the summit of the Paradise Valley trail (go south towards Giant Steps and Sentinel Pass). Climbing another 140 metres, you will have an eye-opening view over Paradise Valley and surroundings mountains.

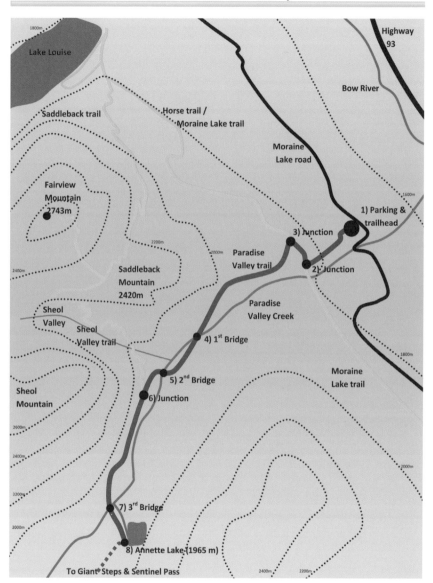

Driving directions

Coming from Lake Louise, take the the Moraine Lake Road for 2.5 km (direction south). The parking lot is situated on the right side of the Moraine Lake Road.

13   Taylor Lake & O'Brien Lake

ROUND-TRIP DISTANCE:	12.4 km
TIME NEEDED:	5 - 6 hrs
ELEVATION GAIN:	600 m
LEVEL:	Moderate
PERIOD:	mid July-September
GEM TREK MAP:	Lake Louise & Yoho

The Taylor Lake trail is located in the northern region of Castle Junction, just southwest of Moraine Lake. This trail is not typically as well trodden as many trails around Lake Louise and Moraine Lake. On this hike, you will enjoy some glorious views on the impressive north face ridges of Mount Bell (to the south). The Taylor Lake trail is a refreshing alternative to the Lake Louise and Moraine Lake trails. During the last few years, the trails in the Moraine Lake area have been subject to numerous group access restrictions or trail closures due to grizzly bear activity in the area. For further information on group access see also Larch Valley trail to Sentinel Pass (hike 9). Hiking restrictions may apply here as well, so always check at the visitor centre at Lake Louise.

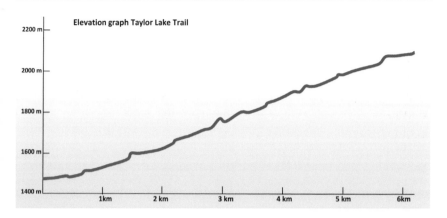

Elevation graph Taylor Lake Trail

Waypoints

1. The Taylor Lake trailhead (elevation level of 1465m) is located at the Taylor Creek Bridge at the south end of the parking area. From the parking area you cross the wooden bridge. The Taylor Lake trail follows the creek up to Taylor Lake in a westward direction.
2. 1.0 km - You cross the 2nd bridge over Taylor Creek.
3. 5.7 km - Cross the 3rd bridge. The trail soon emerges above the tree line. You enter the colourful alpine meadows.
4. 6.0 km - You arrive at a signed junction with the O'Brien Lake trail (left). Continue straight towards Taylor Lake. Note that the trail may be quite muddy in places.
5. 6.2 km - You reach Taylor Lake (elevation level of 2065 metres). Enjoy the great views on Mount Bell to the south and Panorama Ridge to the north. At the north-side of the lake, you find a small tent campground with tables close to the lake, great for a lunch.

From Taylor Lake, there are two possibilities to extend your hike:

1) The Panorama Ridge trail (north):
The trail starts north of the campground. After 500 metres on this steep ascending trail, you will arrive in an area of alpine meadows resplendent with wildflowers. The trail continues from here and remains worthwhile for a few kilometres (the Panorama ridge trail makes a long loop towards Moraine Lake, approximately 10 km further north).

2) The O'Brien Lake trail (south):

The O'Brien Lake is situated only 2 km southeast of Taylor Lake and offers a beautiful addition to your hike. The O'Brien Lake is smaller than Taylor Lake, but the landscape is strewn with meadows brimming with wildflowers. The trail is well defined and not too hard to follow (although not well maintained). To continue to the O'Brien Lake, go back on the trail towards the O'Brien junction (waypoint 4) and turn right. Cross the log bridge over the Taylor Creek. The trail starts descending first, before it starts climbing again (nothing too strenuous). Pay attention as there are a few muddy areas here just before arriving at O'Brien Lake.

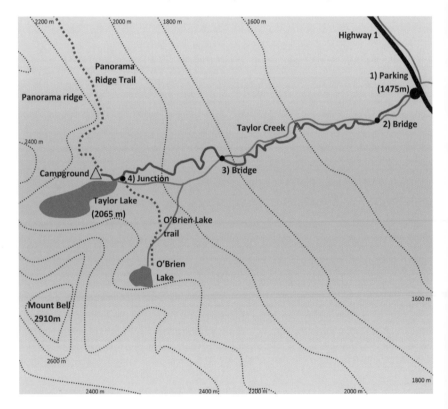

Driving directions

The Taylor Creek Parking is 8 km west of the Castle Junction on the Trans-Canada Highway (Highway 1). The parking is on the southwest side of the road. Be sure to pay attention as there are no signs on the highway for this trail. The trailhead is located at the end of the parking lot.

14   Stanley Glacier

ROUND-TRIP DISTANCE: 9.6 km
TIME NEEDED: 3 hrs
ELEVATION GAIN: 350 m
LEVEL: Easy - Moderate
PERIOD: mid June - end of September
GEM TREK MAP: Kootenay National Park

Stanley Glacier is a short and easy half day hike in the northern part of the Kootenay Natural Park, just south of the border with Banff National Park. The best period to visit this trail is early summer when it magically displays the combination of the melting glacier, great wildflowers and bustlingly powerful streams and waterfalls.

The trail runs through an area that has suffered multiple forest fires in the last ten years. As a result, at places the trees are rather young and not fully grown. This contributes to the open views on your way. Some of the beautiful features on this trail are Stanley Creek and the waterfalls as well as the impressive Stanley Glacier. The small wildlife you may encounter on this hike includes the hoary marmots and pikas (along the scattered rocks). Owing to the milder climate, this trail is usually free of snow early in the season (mid June).

Stanley Glacier

Waypoints

1. From the parking area (elevation level of 1590 metres), you cross the Vermillion Bridge. The trail starts with a steady climb up and follows the Stanley Creek from the south shore.
2. 2 km - It will take you approximately 30 minutes to reach the footbridge across Stanley Creek. From this point on you follow the path along Stanley Creek from the north shore. Soon, the views on Stanley Glacier open up.
3. 4.8 km - You reach the end of the Stanley Glacier trail at the glaciated basin close to the waterfall. A few waterfalls cascade down the cliff walls. Enjoy the great view on Stanley Glacier (elevation level of 1940 metres).

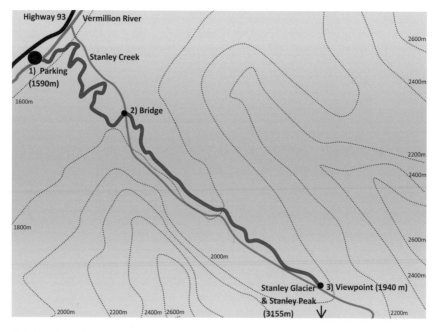

Driving directions

Coming from Banff, take Highway 1 till Castle Junction, then follow Highway 93 south direction Radium Hot Springs. The parking area is just 4 km south of the Alberta/BC border on east side of highway.

15   Johnston Canyon & Inkpots

ROUND-TRIP DISTANCE: Johnston Canyon: 5.6 km

Inkpots: 12 km

TIME NEEDED: Johnston Canyon: 1-2 hrs

Inkpots: 3 - 4 hrs

ELEVATION GAIN: Johnston Canyon: 130 m

Inkpots: 325 m

LEVEL: Johnston Canyon: Very Easy

Inkpots: Moderate

PERIOD: early June - October

GEM TREK MAP: Banff & Mount Assiniboine or Banff - Egypt Lake

Johnston Canyon & Inkpots

Johnston Canyon is probably the most popular destination in the Canadian Rockies and the busiest hiking trail in the Banff area. If you don't like crowds, you may decide to skip this trail, but the Canyon is definitely well worth visiting. It pays off to wake up early in the morning to avoid crowds.

Along the trail you will experience a furious flowing water stream through steep cliffs and rocky walls with a couple of enormous waterfalls. The Canyon has been formed over 350 million years, a period in which the water flow has cut deep through the limestone walls. The walk from the Johnston Canyons to the Inkpots adds diversity and scenic beauty to this hike and is more sublimely attractive for having fewer visitors on the trail. The inkpots are seven small round mineral springs where water bubbles up to the surface.

Waypoints

1. From the parking lot, cross Johnston Creek towards the Johnston Canyon Resort. Turn right at the junction (left is to the resort). From this point on you will remain on the west bank of the Johnston Creek.
2. 1.1 km - You arrive at the viewpoint overlooking the Lower Falls. You can cross a bridge over the creek (to your right) for the best viewpoint. From here, go back and continue on the main trail (north). Soon, you arrive at a junction with a trail leading to Moose Meadows (to your left, 1.5 km). Go straight (north) on the main trail.
3. 2.8 km - You arrive at the Upper Falls viewpoint. A short ascending trail to your right takes you to the elevated viewpoint.
4. 3.3 km - You arrive at another junction (see map) with a trail to Moose Meadows (to the left). The trail to the Inkpots continues in westward direction, then gradually curving north. It is another 2.7 km to the inkpots. The trail continues with a moderate climb until you reach the summit of the trail (elevation 1750 metres). Thereafter you gradually descend (to 1650 metres) and soon enter the open meadows.
5. 6.0 km - You arrive at the Inkpots a great place for a picnic and to enjoy the scenic beauty. Take the same route back.

Johnston Canyon & Inkpots

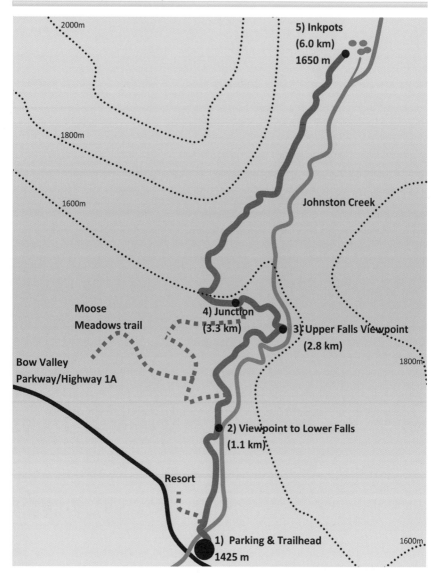

Driving directions

Take the Bow Valley Parkway (Highway 1A) to Johnston Canyon (18 km northwest of Banff). The parking is on the eastside of Johnston Creek. From the parking, you cross the bridge over Johnston Creek to the Johnston Creek Resort and trailhead (westside of the creek).

16 Bourgeau Lake - Mount Bourgeau

ROUND-TRIP DISTANCE: Bourgeau Lake: 15 km
       Mount Bourgeau: 24 km
TIME NEEDED: Bourgeau Lake: 5 hrs
       Mount Bourgeau: 8 hrs
ELEVATION GAIN: Bourgeau Lake: 710 m
       Mount Bourgeau: 1490 m
LEVEL: Bourgeau Lake: Challenging
       Mount Bourgeau: Strenuous
PERIOD: early July - end of September
MAP: Banff Up - close

Bourgeau Lake and Mount Bourgeau are absolutely fabulous destinations. The stretch from Bourgeau Lake to Mount Bourgeau is the most stunning, but also the most arduous stretch of hiking. This hike and the Cory Pass - Mount Edith loop are the two most strenuous and lengthy day hikes within close vicinity of Banff, providing a panoply of Banff National Park with all its great mountains, peaks and valleys. We advise anyone planning on taking this hike to check on the weather and trail conditions at the visitor centre in Banff.

Bourgeau Lake - Mount Bourgeau

For a less difficult and strenuous alternative you might choose to walk only the first part to Bourgeau Lake or the Harvey Pass viewpoint (9.6 km). The Bourgeau Lake hike takes about 2.5 hours (one way) and is a highly rewarding hike. At the majestic amphitheatre at Bourgeau Lake the views are great. There is no short-age of pikas and chipmunks hopping around as they tend to gather under the rocks and stones.

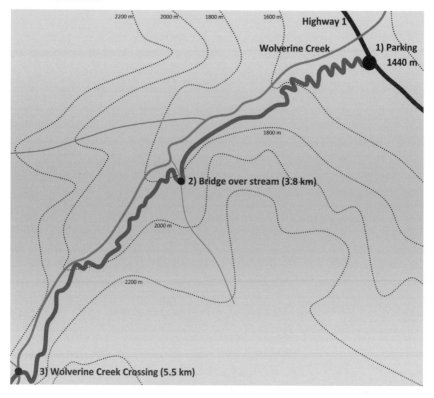

From the trailhead to the Wolverine Creek Crossing

Waypoints to Bourgeau Lake

1. At the south end of the parking lot, you will see a steel fence designed to protect the wildlife. The trailhead starts here. After a few minutes walk-ing, the trail steadily ascends (with switchbacks). As the trail is well pre-pared, the walk up is not too arduous.

2. 3.8 km - You cross a small stream with a wooden bridge (from time to time, you may not see any water flowing).

3. 5.5 km - You arrive at the crossing with the Wolverine Creek. The trail levels out as you enter the open meadows before arriving at the lake.
4. 7.5 km - You reach Bourgeau Lake (2150 metres). Mount Bourgeau is towering on you left.

Bourgeau Lake

Bourgeau Lake to Mount Bourgeau

In case you decide to continue to Mount Bourgeau, you follow the Harvey Pass trail that starts in the north corner of Bourgeau Lake. The higher levels of this trail may be covered in snow until early summer. Never go up this trail when it is covered with snow or ice.

While you will experience magnificent views all the way up to Harvey Pass, you cannot compare those views with the wonders to be experienced at the summit of Mount Bourgeau. Here, you will have a brilliant 360 degree panoramic view which includes the town of Banff (you need to look northeast up the Trans-Canada Highway past the Vermillion lakes), the Bow River Valley and a top view on Bourgeau Lake. Total distance from the trailhead is 12 km with 1435 metres elevation gain.

Bourgeau Lake - Mount Bourgeau

Waypoints to Mount Bourgeau

Follow the Harvey Pass trail at the northeast corner of the lake which ascends in a westerly direction on a slippery, rocky path. Be very careful when climbing up.

5. 8.7 km - You arrive at a mountain top shaped like a bowl embracing a small mountain lake. You pass the mountain lake on its north shore. Within a few minutes you pass a small stream coming from another small mountain lake (see map).

6. 9.6 km - You arrive at Harvey Lake & Harvey Pass (2450 metres). The views just get better and better. Looking south, you will see Mount Assiniboine. From here, it is another 2.4 km and another 480 metres elevation gain to Mount Bourgeau. It is absolutely worthwhile but you should have enough time and feel fit enough. The panorama is fantastic from the summit. It takes you approximately another hour to go up and then about 3.5 hours to walk back to the parking lot. Take the trail on your left (uphill). It feels like an endless scramble on this ridge to the summit of Mount Bourgeau.

7. 12.0 km - You arrive at the summit of Mount Bourgeau (2930 metres!).

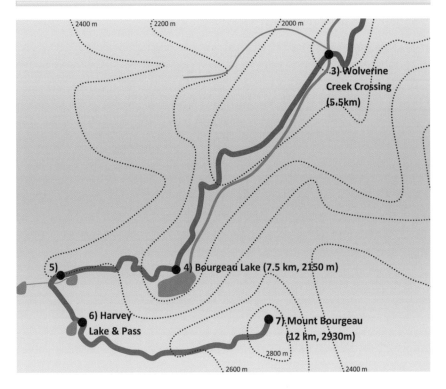

From Wolverine Creek crossing to Mount Bourgeau

Driving directions

The trailhead of the Bourgeau Lake trail is located on the Trans-Canada Highway approximately 15 km west of the Town of Banff. The parking is on the south side of the four lane divided highway.

17   Cory Pass - Mount Edith Loop

ROUND-TRIP DISTANCE: 13.2 km
TIME NEEDED: 6 hrs
ELEVATION GAIN: 910 m
LEVEL: Strenuous
PERIOD: mid July - end of September
GEM TREK MAP: Banff Up - close

Cory Pass - Mount Edith Loop, located only 5 km from the town of Banff, will provide a genuine taste of the spectacular nature in this part of the Canadian Rockies. This hike will take you to stunning views of the beautiful surrounding mountains, like Mount Edith and Mount Louis. Cory Pass - Mount Edith Loop and the trail to Bourgeau Lake - Mount Bourgeau are the two most impressive, strenuous day hikes within the vicinity of the town of Banff.

Please be aware that this trail is not for the inexperienced hiker at it is steep, especially at the start of the loop on the Cory Pass trail (see elevation graph around the 2 km point). There are also a few difficult parts where you should take extra care. It can be windy and chilly on top of Mount Edith, so ensure you take enough warm clothes. It becomes hazardous to hike here when there is snow or ice (slippery) on the trail. We advise anyone planning to hike here to check the weather and trail conditions at the visitor centre in Banff.

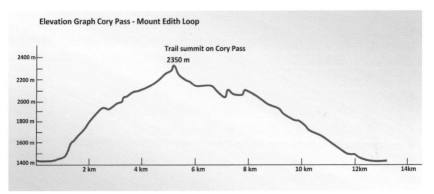

Note: The Cory Pass - Mount Edith Loop combines two trails. You start on the Cory Pass trail for the first 9 km. Then you continue on the Edith Pass trail till the end of the Mount Edith Loop (waypoints 2 & 5 in map).

Cory Pass - Mount Edith Loop

Waypoints

1. You find the trailhead of this hike at the far end of the picnic area. From the parking area, you cross the bridge and pass the picnic area. Turn right (easterly direction) on an old fire road for about 250 metres and then go left (marked with a signpost).

2. 1.2 km - You arrive at the junction of the Mount Edith Loop. Take the trail on your left (Cory Pass trail) and go clockwise around Mount Edith. Be prepared for an arduous hike up. You soon arrive at a rocky, steep ridge. Here, you will be able to enjoy the first great panoramic views with Mount Edith to the north and Mount Bourgeau to the southwest (on the other side of Highway 1).

3. 5.9 km - You arrive at Cory Pass (elevation level of 2350 metres), the summit of this loop. Here you have a great view on majestic Mount Louis (and Mount Edith). From here, the trail continues with a gradual ascent over rocky terrain. In about 15 minutes (from Cory Pass) you arrive at a small rocky cliff above the Gargoyle Valley (see map) where you need to use your hands to balance yourself for a safe climb down (nothing too difficult, just take care).

4. 9.0 km - You arrive at a junction with the Edith Pass trail. Take the trail on your right (south, descending). The left trail goes to the Forty Mile Creek (north). From here, you descend along the creek.

5. 12.0 km - You return to the first junction of the Cory Pass trail and Edith Pass trail.

6. 13.2 km - You have completed the trail on your return to the parking area.

Driving directions

Coming from Banff, take the Trans-Canada Highway (Highway 1) exit towards the Bow Valley Parkway (Highway 1A) approximately 5.5 km from the town of Banff. Continue on the Bow Valley Parkway for 0.5 km. Then turn right on the signed road that leads to the Fireside Picnic area.

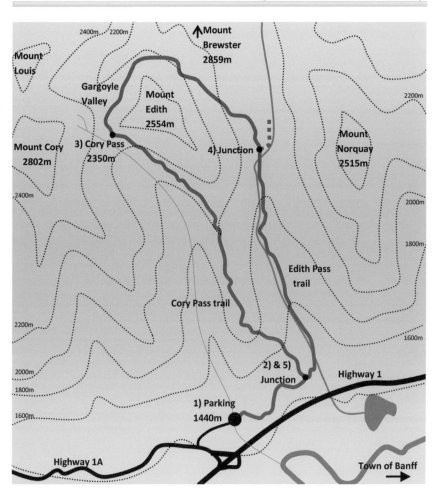

18   C-Level Cirque

ROUND-TRIP DISTANCE:	8.4 km
TIME NEEDED:	3 - 4 hrs
ELEVATION GAIN:	465 m
LEVEL:	Moderate
PERIOD:	mid June - end of September
GEM TREK MAP:	Banff Up - close

View on the glacier from the Cirque (end of September)

C-Level Cirque is located on the eastside of the Cascade Mountains close to the Town of Banff. It is not a long hike and the trail is rather clear without any major difficulty. C-Level Cirque is a good choice in case you visit the Town of Banff a couple of days and you look for a short moderate hike nearby. The first part of the trail you steadily walk up through a nice mixed forest of spruce, pine and aspen with quite a few wildflowers along the trail. As you climb up, you pass a few fenced off ventilation shafts from the old coal mine that used to be operational back in the early 1920's. "C-Level" is a reference to the elevation level of the old coal mine that used to operate here. From the viewpoint at the Cirque amphitheatre you will enjoy a great view on Lake Minnewanka and the surrounding mountains, situated just east of the Cirque.

Waypoints

1. At the parking lot (elevation level of 1465 metres) you will see the trail-head to the left of the information board (on the west side of the parking area). The trail, an old coal mining access road, is very wide and in good condition. The first 45 minutes you walk uphill through a forest of pine, aspen and spruce trees.

2. 1.1 km - You will pass the remainders of a small C-Level coal mine-house.

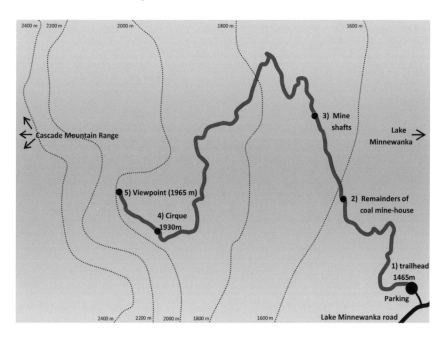

3. 1.9 km - You pass a few mineshaft ventilation holes (deep holes in the ground that are sign-posted and fenced). After approximately 3.5 km steadily climbing up over the steep ridge, the views open up. You will be able to see the Town of Banff, Bow Valley, Mount Rundle and quite a few other beautiful lakes and mountain tops.

C-Level Cirque

4. 3.9 km - You reach the Cirque, where the trees are replaced with dramatic rocky scenery and you have great views of the cliffs and glaciers of the Cascade Mountains. You may catch sight of pikas and even hoary marmots at the rocks and boulders (sit down at the boulders and wait quietly). To the right side of the cirque you will see a trail that leads to a short walk uphill for an additional 300 metres to an even more elevated viewpoint.
5. 4.2 km - You arrive at the elevated viewpoint on the right side of the cirque. Enjoy the great view on among others Lake Minnewanka, Bow Valley and the Three Sisters. Take the same route back.

At the Cirque with cloudy weather. To the right you see the trail going up to the most elevated viewpoint.

Driving directions

Coming from Banff, take the Lake Minnewanka Road (direction north). Continue on the Lake Minnewanka Road for approximately 3.5 km (1 km before you will arrive at Lake Minnewanka). You will find the Upper Bankhead Picnic Area to your left (coming from Banff).

19   Lake Minnewanka

ROUND-TRIP DISTANCE:	15 km
TIME NEEDED:	3 - 4 hrs
ELEVATION GAIN:	40 m
LEVEL:	Easy
PERIOD:	mid June - early October
GEM TREK MAP:	Banff up-close

This trail on the north shore of Lake Minnewanka is perfect for a relaxed and easy-going half day hike in a beautiful setting. This trail is also a great place for a family with young children to visit.

Lake Minnewanka, also named Devil's Lake by the First Nations, is one of the deepest and largest lakes of the Canadian Rockies. The deep water gives the lake its intense dark blue color. The current Lake Minnewanka dam that was built in 1942 is almost 24 km long and 142 metres deep. Lake Minnewanka is the only lake in Banff National Park where motorized boats are allowed. It is also a great place for backcountry camping and fishing.

Lake Minnewanka

The first 7.5 km of the trail to the Aylmer junction is very popular. From there, a very beautiful destination is the elevated Aylmer Lookout (2040 m) where the views on Lake Minnewanka are fabulous. However the Aylmer Pass trail enters an active grizzly bear habitat. From mid July till the end of October, the bears are attracted by the many Buffalo- and Grouse berries in the area. Parks Canada regulations still may allow you to enter the area with group access restrictions (see also Hike 9, Larch Valley to Sentinel Pass), however our suggestion is not to disturb the bears and not to hike up the Aylmer Pass trail during the berry season. As an alternative, the Lake Minnewanka trail continues for many kilometres along the lake towards the other backcountry campgrounds.

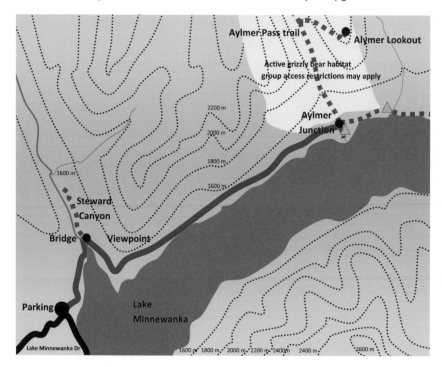

Waypoints

1. The trailhead for the Lake Minnewanka trail is located at the far end of the picnic area. From the parking lot you walk in a north-easterly direction and will find the trailhead sign at the end of the pavement. The trail starts on a wide, accessible path.

2. 0.9 km - You cross the Steward Canyon Bridge and pass the canyon on

your left. After crossing the bridge, you pass a junction with a trail to Steward Canyon (left). Ignore this trail and continue on the Lake Minnewanka trail curving south.

3. 2.5 km - You arrive at an elevated viewpoint on Lake Minnewanka (elevation level of 1525 metres). From here, the trail starts descending as you continue to walk east, parallel to the lakeshore.

4. 7.3 km - You arrive at a junction with the campground on your right and the trail to Aylmer Pass on your left. This is a great place for a rest or a picnic. Enjoy the scenery. It is also a good turning point for a day hike. You may see quite a few hikers that continue to one of the backcountry campgrounds along Lake Minnewanka.

Driving directions

From the Trans-Canada Highway (Highway 1), take exit Banff East to the Lake Minnewanka Road (direction north). After 5 km you arrive at the parking lot of Lake Minnewanka.

20   Helen Lake & Katherine Lake

ROUND-TRIP DISTANCE: Helen Lake: 12 km
                            Katherine Lake: 16.2 km
TIME NEEDED: Helen Lake: 4 - 5 hrs
                            Katherine Lake: 5 - 6 hrs
ELEVATION GAIN: Helen Lake: 425 m
                            Katherine Lake: 675 m
LEVEL: Moderate
PERIOD: early July - end of September
GEM TREK MAP: Bow Lake - Saskatchewan Crossing

This hike is a real gem during the milder season: meadows full of wildflowers, blue lakes, high peaks and a remarkable alpine landscape. Best time to hike is the early summer when the wildflower colours are flourishing. The Helen Lake trail is unsurprisingly popular as it takes you into the colourful alpine meadows before reaching beautiful Helen Lake and Katherine Lake. Do not be shocked to see plenty of hoary marmots when you enter the colourful meadows. The trail from Helen Lake to Katherine Lake (2.1 km one way) is the perfect addition to spend more time in this beautiful part of the Canadian Rockies.

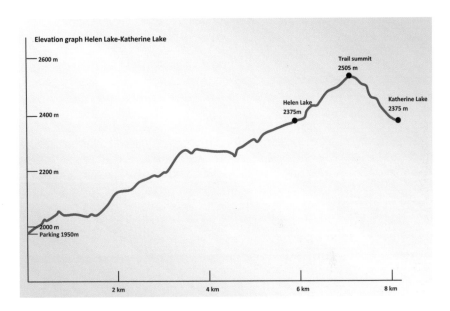

Waypoints

1. From the start of the trail you walk east for the first 2.5 km. The trail gradually ascends through a beautiful sub-alpine forest.
2. 2.5 km - The views slowly open up as you enter the elevated alpine meadows. Looking southwest, you can see Crowfoot Mountain and Bow Lake. When you approach the southeast end of a lateral moraine, the trail gradually curves north (around the 3 km point).
3. 5.0 km - About 500 metres after passing a rockslide you arrive at Helen Creek. Look for the best spot to cross the creek so as to keep your feet dry. From here, you soon enter a beautiful open alpine landscape with rocky meadows and mountain peaks.

4. 6.0 km - You arrive at Helen Lake (2375 metres) located at the foot of Cirque Peak with an impressive height of 2993 metres. If you have enough stamina and would like to add another 2.1 km (one way) to this beautiful hike, you can continue to Katherine Lake by heading north and climbing another 130 metres over the next kilometre.

5. 7.0 km - You reach the summit of the trail at 2505 metres with great views in all directions. On your left you see a trail that goes up Cirque Peak. From the summit the trail descends all the way to Katherine Lake.

6. 8.1 km - You reach Katherine Lake (2375 metres). Katherine Lake is a great destination with great views of the southern mountain ranges. Take the same route back.

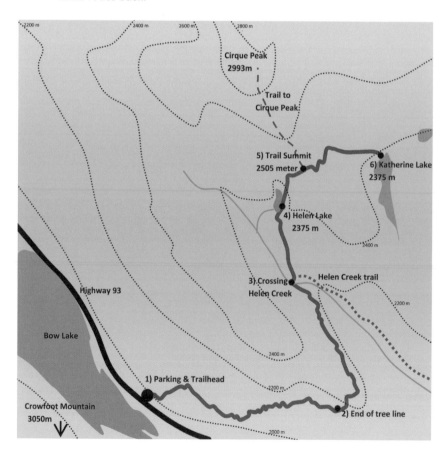

Driving directions

The parking area for the Helen Lake trail is located on the Icefield parkway (Highway 93), approximately 33 km northwest of the Lake Louise junction. The parking is on the other side of the Crowfoot Glacier Viewpoint. The Crowfoot Glacier Viewpoint is clearly sign posted on the highway.

21   Bow Glacier Falls

ROUND-TRIP DISTANCE: 9.2 km
TIME NEEDED: 3 hrs
ELEVATION GAIN: 145 m
LEVEL: Easy
PERIOD: July - early October
GEM TREK MAP: Bow Lake & Saskatchewan Crossing

Bow Glacier Falls is a short but incredibly rewarding hike. This trail halfway between Lake Louise and the Jasper-Banff boundary offers really fantastic scenery.
You will enjoy the beautiful view when passing the turquoise coloured Bow Lake
with the majestic crowfoot mountain as its backdrop. The highlight of the trail
is of course the 120 metres high Bow Glacier Falls. The best time to see the Bow
Lake Falls is on the warmest day in the summer when the ice melting is at its
peak. This is a relatively easy hike as most of the trail is without major elevation
gain across an occasionally undulating landscape. The trail is from time to time a
bit muddy and slippery. Pay attention when you arrive at the steep rocky gorge
(3.4 km), especially when the trail is wet or covered with ice or snow.

Waypoints

1. From the parking area, walk towards the Num-Ti-Jah Lodge. The trail starts here. Elevation level of the trailhead is 1925 metres. The trail follows the Bow Lake shoreline to its west corner and starts on a very clear, wide and flat pathway until the end of the lake. From here, the trail is more rugged heading towards the falls. Depending on the time of the year, you may pass a little stream flowing towards Bow Lake (see map).

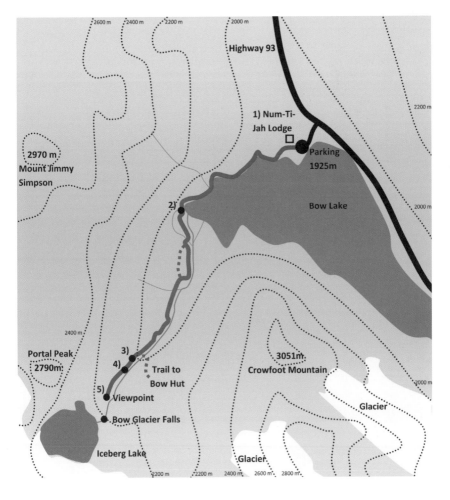

2. 1.8 km - You arrive at the west corner of Bow Lake. From here, the trail follows the stream that flows from the glacier to Bow Lake

Bow Glacier Falls

(stream is to your left). You may notice another path that runs parallel to this trail. Both trails merge again a little further on.

3. 3.3 km - The trail starts ascending towards a steep rocky gorge. Be careful here as it may be slippery when wet or covered with snow or ice. A little further, the trail continues its ascent over a terminal moraine.

4. 3.7 km - You reach the crest of the terminal moraine. Follow the cairns (pile or stack of rocks used to indicate the route). The trail descends towards the basin of the falls.

5. 4.7 km - You arrive at the viewpoint on Bow Glacier Falls (elevation level of 2070 metres). Take the same route back.

Driving directions

You find the parking of Bow Glacier Falls on the north side of Bow Lake, halfway between Lake Louise and the Jasper-Banff boundary. Take the exit to the Num-Ti-Jah Lodge (on your left coming from Banff, on your right coming from Jasper). The parking area is located on the southwest side of the road.

22   Bow Summit Lookout

ROUND-TRIP DISTANCE:	6.2 km
TIME NEEDED:	2 hrs
ELEVATION GAIN:	230 m
LEVEL:	Easy
PERIOD:	July - end of September
GEM TREK MAP:	Bow Lake - Saskatchewan Crossing

This short and easy hike on the old fire lookout road to Bow Summit offers great views of Caldron Peak and the Peyto Valley. From this summit you also have the best panorama views on the famous Peyto Lake and Bow Lake. The trail starts at the popular viewpoint on Peyto Lake. Since the parking for this hike is at an elevated level of 2085 m, you only have to climb 230 meter to get to this fabulous viewpoint. For the best experience, do not stop at the Peyto Lake viewpoint, but continue directly to the Bow Summit Lookout. This hike will only take about 2 hours, therefore a great hike to combine or as an in-between. The alpine meadows and wildflowers will undoubtedly compliment your panoramic appreciation.

Waypoints

1. From the Bow Summit parking area (elevation level of 2085 metres), you follow the sign-posted trail down to the Peyto Lake viewing point. This first part is straightforward and the walk is normally well populated.

2. 0.6 km - You reach the famous viewpoint on Peyto Lake. From here, continue on the main trail and walk uphill. You pass a trail (to your right) after approximately 50 metres which leads to Peyto Lake and Caldron

Lake (downhill). Continue on the main trail for another 100 metres.

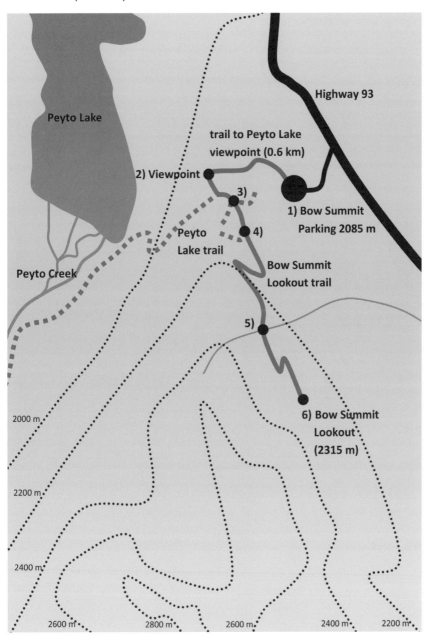

Bow Summit Lookout

3. 0.7 km - You arrive at a 3-way junction. Continue straight (which is the middle path). The trail starts climbing with a gradual ascent.
4. 0.9 km - You reach another junction (paved trail turns to the right). Walk straight ahead on the old fire lookout road. The trail meanders up. The views on the valley get better and better as you reach the higher grounds.
5. 2.6 km - The trail shortly descends untill you arrive at a small stream, where you have a good chance to spot hoary marmots. The trail starts climbing again after the stream.
6. 3.1 km - You arrive at Bow Summit Lookout (elevation level of 2315 m).

Driving directions

On the Icefield Parkway, the parking area is located 4.9 km north of the Num-Ti-Jah Lodge, just north of Bow Lake. Parking is on the west side of the road at the end of the Peyto Lake Viewpoint Access Road.

23   Caldron Lake

ROUND-TRIP DISTANCE: 15.6 km
TIME NEEDED: 7 - 8 hrs
ELEVATION GAIN: 905 m
LEVEL: Strenuous
PERIOD: July - end of September
GEM TREK MAP: Bow Lake - Saskatchewan Crossing

The Caldron Lake trail is a fabulous hike with fantastic views. The hike starts at the busy viewpoint where everyone visiting the Canadian Rockies makes a fabulous picture of beautiful Peyto Lake. This trail is not officially maintained by Parks Canada – one possible reason as to why it is not used by so many hikers. Please note that the trail is not clearly signposted all the way up to Caldron Lake. This hike requires some more attention along your way and some route finding skills. For the majority of the route, it should not be too hard to find your way, as the trail follows the Peyto Creek upstream. Please ensure you are equipped with a good compass and a map of this region.

Caldron Lake

Waypoints

1. From the parking area (elevation level of 2070 metres), you follow the sign-posted trail to the Peyto Lake viewing point. This is a straightforward and usually crowded walk (0.6 km).

2. 0.6 km - You arrive at the famous viewpoint on beautiful Peyto Lake (elevation level of 2135 metres). From here, go back to the main trail and turn right. After 50 metres, take another right turn on a descending trail leading to the level of Peyto Lake. Be careful as the trail descends steeply at some points. It will take you about 30 to 40 minutes to reach the Peyto Lake shore (elevation level of 1850 metres). Do not go to the lake but stay on the trail that curves left (in a south-westerly direction).

3. 3.2 km - The path is not well sign-posted from this point on. Go southwest, following the riverbed of the Peyto Creek and keep it to your right. As you walk along the creek, you may be able to see the lateral moraine which will be the path up (approximately 2.5 km further). Follow the cairned pathway.

4. 5.5 km - You come to a rather narrow, cabled log bridge. Cross Peyto Creek here. Note that you are now still south of the Caldron Creek (see map).

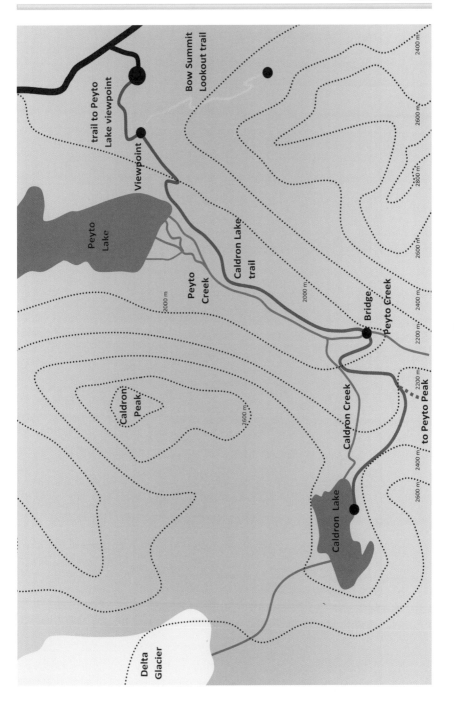

Caldron Lake

Directly after crossing the Peyto Creek, you turn right (in a north-erly direction). First, the trail goes downstream for a few hundred metres before the trail starts climbing and curving west. You soon ascend to the lower part of a lateral moraine of Peyto Peak. It is a steep climb. Do not continue at this point when this trail is covered with snow. In this case, it is strongly recommended that you go back as it certainly will become more slippery and potentially dangerous at the higher level ridges.

5. As you approach the top of the ridge (elevation level of 2410 metres) the trail splits up in two. Take the path on the right towards Caldron Lake (the other trail goes in a southerly direction to Peyto Peak). The trail soon starts descending to the lake and curves north-westerly. The lake falls within your vision only minutes before arrival.

6. 7.8 km - You arrive at Caldron Lake (elevation level of 2350 m). Take the same route back.

Driving directions

Follow Highway 93 to the Peyto Lake viewpoint parking area 4.9 km north of the Num-Ti-Jah Lodge (north of Bow Lake).

24   Nigel Pass

ROUND-TRIP DISTANCE:	14.4 km
TIME NEEDED:	4 - 5 hrs round trip
ELEVATION GAIN:	365 m
LEVEL:	Moderate
PERIOD:	mid July - September
GEM TREK MAP:	Columbia Icefield

Nigel Pass is one of the best longer day hikes in the Columbia Icefield area. Nigel pass is a much less crowded trail than Parker Ridge or Wilcox pass, both trails only a few miles away from Nigel Pass. Nigel Pass is a truly beautiful place to visit, a jewel amongst the cornucopia of pleasures provided by the Rockies.

The Nigel Pass trail follows the Nigel Creek till the boundary of the Banff- and Jasper National Park. The open scenery during the majority of the trail gives you a feeling of being completely submerged in a vast gigantic landscape with majestic views everywhere you look. Enjoy the sensation when you are far away from the highway, in the middle of the elevated valley surrounded by the massive mountain peaks, including to the south Mount Saskatchewan and Mount Athabasca.

Nigel Pass

The beautiful open meadows along the route will be filled with vibrant coloured flowers in the early summer season. The Nigel Pass trail is long but will be easily managed by most hikers. The final 2 kilometres before reaching Nigel Pass will require the greatest effort.

Waypoints

1. From the parking area (elevation level of 1860 metres), walk down the gravel road for 100 metres until you see the trailhead and information board on the right side of the road. Cross the bridge over Nigel Creek. The trail starts through a small open forest. After approximately 45 minutes you pass a couple of junctions (not all that clear) with a trail to the left. Ignore these and continue straight on the main trail. Keep Nigel Creek to your left and continue in a northerly direction. Soon, you enter the open meadows.

2. 2.1 km - You pass the site of the Historic Camp Parker. This is the place where the first hunters used to camp when they were out hunting in this area. Note the carvings on the trees around the camp.

3. 5.2 km - You arrive at a junction with a horse trail to the left. Ignore this trail and continue walking north on the same trail. The trail becomes somewhat more arduous as the trail heads uphill.

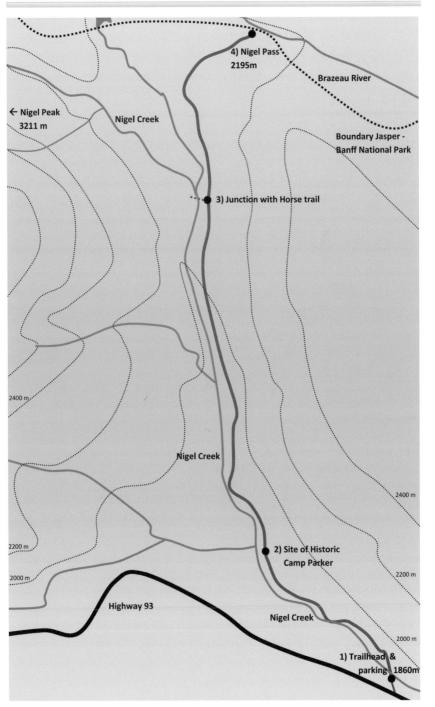

4) Nigel Pass
2195m

Brazeau River

← Nigel Peak
3211 m

Nigel Creek

Boundary Jasper -
Banff National Park

3) Junction with Horse trail

2400 m

Nigel Creek

2400 m

2200 m

2) Site of Historic
Camp Parker

2200 m

2000 m

Highway 93

Nigel Creek

2000 m

1) Trailhead &
parking 1860m

4. 7.2 km - As the trail levels out, you arrive at the trail summit at Nigel Pass, close to the Jasper- and Banff National Park boundary and also close to the Brazeau River (2195 m). From here, take the same route back.

Driving directions

The parking area for the Nigel Pass trail is located on Highway 93, approximately 8 km south of the Jasper-Banff boundary (at Sunwapta Pass) on the right side of the road coming from Banff or on the left side coming from Jasper. Look for the sign "Nigel Creek / Ruisseau Nigel".

25   Parker Ridge

ROUND-TRIP DISTANCE:	5.6 km
TIME NEEDED:	2 hrs
ELEVATION GAIN:	250 m
LEVEL:	Easy
BEST PERIOD:	mid July - September
GEM TREK MAP:	Columbia Icefield

Parker Ridge is the most popular trail in the Columbia Icefield area. It is a short but marvellous hike and worth every effort. It will take you only about 2 hours in total, providing great views of the 9 km-long Saskatchewan Glacier and the surrounding peaks.

It is very convenient that the trailhead starts at a level of 2000 m, so you only have to climb up 250 metres to reach the summit at Parker Ridge. Before you even realize it, you have reached the summit. Probably the best timing to hike if you prefer solitude is in the early morning or some-what later in the day. You may well see bighorn sheep, pikas and mountain goats on the ridges and slopes. Note that Parks Canada usually keeps the trail closed in the early season until the trail is dry enough for hiking.

Parker Ridge

Waypoints

1. From the trailhead at the southside of parking area, you enter a forest of subalpine fir and Engelmann spruce. You steadily meander up and you will submerge from the tree line after approximately 1 km. From here, the views open up as you enter the alpine meadow.

2. 2.1 km - You arrive at the summit of the Parker ridge. The trail continues to your left (southeast direction, see map) of the ridge. Continue for another 700 metres to the best viewpoint of the Saskatchewan Glacier, the largest ice field south of the Arctic Circle.

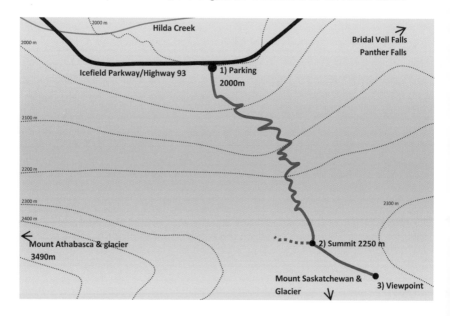

3. 2.8 km - You arrive at a marvellous viewpoint on the Saskatchewan Glacier. From here you can explore some of the other short pathways on the summit to alternative viewpoints. Return the way you came.

Driving directions

The parking lot of Parker Ridge is located on Highway 93, 4 km south of the Banff-Jasper boundary (Sunwapta Pass), on the southwest side of the road.

26   Wilcox Pass

ROUND-TRIP DISTANCE:	8 km
TIME NEEDED:	3 hrs
ELEVATION GAIN:	355 m
LEVEL:	Moderate
PERIOD:	mid July - end of September
GEM TREK MAP:	Columbia Icefield

Wilcox Pass is a beautiful hike and everyone visiting the Canadian Rockies should see it. The hike to the summit on Wilcox Pass takes you only 1.5 hours (one way). The trail takes you up into a beautiful alpine valley between Nigel Peak and Mount Wilcox. The views are stunning at the higher levels of this alpine valley. Wilcox Pass is usually a rather busy trail due to its proximity to the Athabasca Glacier and two campgrounds (Columbia Icefield and Wilcox Creek Campground). On this hike, you are most likely to see the beautiful bighorn sheep grazing on the slopes and ridges.

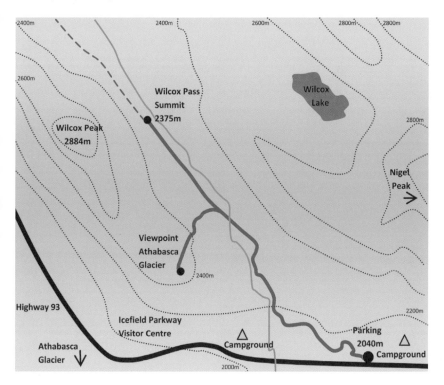

Waypoints

1. The trailhead of the Wilcox Pass is close to the Wilcox Creek campground on the left side of the campground access road. From the trailhead (2040 m), the trail heads uphill (quite steeply) and passes an old subalpine forest.

Wilcox Pass

2. 2 km - You reach the tree line and enter the open meadows. Great views open up.

3. 4 km - You reach the summit of Wilcox Pass (2375 metres) which provides the best views of the surrounding peaks and glaciers including Mount Athabasca. From here, you can also decide to keep walking in this direction for a while (north-westerly) as the trail continues for another 7 km to Tangle Creek. You can also go back and continue towards the side trail (see map) to another great viewpoint on the Athabasca Glacier (south-westerly direction).

Driving directions

The Parking area for the Wilcox Pass trail is located on Highway 93, approximately 1 km southeast of the Jasper-Banff Boundary (at Sunwapta Pass) on the right side of the road coming from Banff or on the left side coming from Jasper.

27   Cavell Meadows

ROUND-TRIP DISTANCE:	8.0 km
TIME NEEDED:	2 - 3 hrs
ELEVATION GAIN:	400 m for Cavell Meadows loop
	520 m to highest viewpoint
LEVEL:	Moderate
PERIOD:	mid July - September
GEM TREK MAP:	Jasper - Maligne Lake

This trail is definitely one of the top 10 best day hikes in the Canadian Rockies and probably for that reason also one of the most popular trails in Jasper National Park. When you arrive at the parking area, you probably see quite a few cars; however note that most visitors just walk the short interpretive loop (Path of the Glacier) to Angel Glacier and Cavell Pond. The Path of the Glacier trail requires minimal effort (only 1.6 km long) and is a great choice if you look for an easy stroll rather than a moderate - arduous hike.

Both trails will show you the astonishing views and sounds of Angel Glacier. At the base of Angel Glacier you will find Cavell Pond, a cold-water lake that is fed by the glacier. Cavell Pond is famous for its huge icebergs, sometimes as big as houses, floating in the small lake. The Cavell Meadows trail takes you up to the

Cavell Meadows

flower-filled meadows in a beautiful valley just east of the peak of Mount Edith Cavell and Angel Glacier. The trail is especially loved for the full range of floral colors on display in addition to the already astonishing scenery of the mountains. You will probably see the occasional marmot in the rocky areas of the trail as well as some caribou herds, in the lower parts of the hills. Note that on this trail, you are not allowed to take any dogs as they may disturb the caribou herds. The trail normally opens early – mid July depending on the weather as the alpine meadows need to be snow free and dry enough for walking. The trail closes around the end of September. The friends of Jasper did a great job in 2002-2004 to restore this beautiful trail, so please stay on the trails and follow the official marked routes.

Waypoints

1. Follow the Path of the Glacier trail on the south-western corner of the parking lot. This trail is the shortest route to the Cavell Meadows loop. As the pavement ends, the trail continues on a dirt road.

2. 0.5 km - You arrive at the junction with the Cavell Meadows trail (left). Go left here. (*Note: The Path of the Glacier trail turns right and passes Cavell Pond making a 1.8 km loop returning to the parking lot.*) The trail steadily climbs uphill with a few switchbacks. You will pass

some rocky areas where you may encounter small wildlife like hoary marmots and pikas.

3. 2.0 km - You arrive at a junction with the Cavell Meadows loop. Take the trail on your right. Within a few hundred metres, you reach a nice elevated viewpoint on Angel Glacier and Mount Edith Cavell. The views open up as you enter the beautiful alpine meadows.
4. 2.8 km - You reach the most southern junction of the Cavell Meadows loop. For another great viewpoint, go right here for 100 metres. To continue, return to the junction and continue on the Cavell Meadows loop (coming from the viewpoint, it is the trail on your right going in a northerly direction, see map).
5. 3.0 km - You pass a junction with a shortcut trail to the left (dotted, black line on map). Continue on the Cavell Meadows trail (right).
6. 3.5 km - You arrive at a junction with a trail (to your right) which leads to the most elevated viewpoint of this trail. It is an arduous climb up for about 400 metres with another elevation gain of 120 metres.
7. 3.9 km - From the viewpoint (2280 metres), return to the junction (waypoint 6) and continue on the Cavell Meadows loop (right trail).
8. 4.7 km - You pass the shortcut trail on your left (black, dotted line on map).
9. 6.0 km - You return to the start of the Cavell Meadows loop.
10. 7.5 km - You are back at the junction with the Path of the Glacier trail. Go left here if you prefer to take the longer loop back via Cavell Pond. Go right for the shortest route to the parking area.
11. 8.0 km - You return at the parking area.

Driving directions

Coming from Jasper (or Highway 16), take Highway 93 for approximately 6 km and then continue on Highway 93A for approximately 6 km. Take a right turn onto the Cavell road and continue on this road for 15 km until you arrive at the Cavell Meadows parking lot. Note that the road is not suited for vehicles larger than 7 metres long due to the tight, narrow switchbacks in the road.

Cavell Meadows

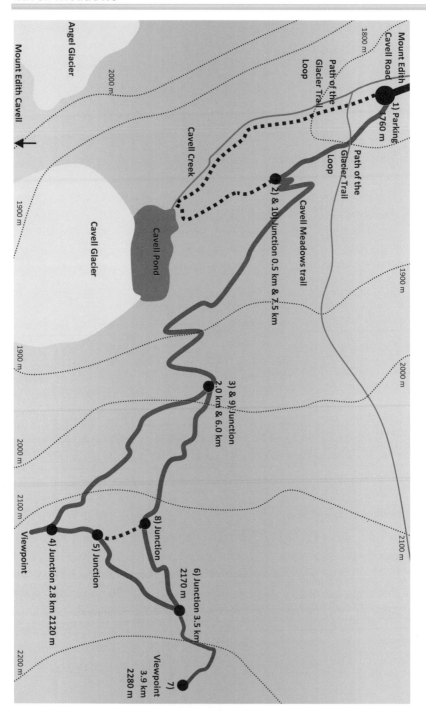

28   Bald Hills

ROUND-TRIP DISTANCE: 13.4 km
TIME NEEDED: 4 - 5 hrs
ELEVATION GAIN: 630 m
LEVEL: Challenging
PERIOD: July - September
GEM TREK MAP: Jasper - Maligne Lake

Bald Hills at Lake Maligne is an outstanding hike in Jasper National Park. The trail is basically a former fire lookout road, leading to higher grounds where the views on Maligne Lake and the Queen Elisabeth mountain ranges (north side of Maligne Lake) are astonishing.

This hike can be quite strenuous, especially during wet conditions. Don't be mis-led as the first 2 kilometres are surely not the most impressive. However the scenery completely changes as soon as you arrive in the beautiful open alpine meadows. It can be such a joyful hike, especially when the summer wildflowers are flourishing. This is also the best time to spot a caribou herd in the lower parts of these hills. To prevent the disturbance of these caribou herds, no dogs are al-lowed in this area.

Bald Hills

Waypoints

1. The trailhead (elevation level of 1690 metres) is on the west side of the parking lot at the gated fire road which is well sign-posted. The trail starts off through an open forest. Within approximately 350 metres you pass a trail on your left leading to Moose Lake and Maligne Pass (see map). Continue your hike up on the wide old fire road.

2. 2.6 km - As the scenery changes and you enter the alpine meadows, you will approach the Bald Hills Loop junction. At this point you can decide to take the short route up (dotted line on map, left trail), which is a steeper route or you can take the longer and easier route (right trail). We prefer the longer route for an easier climb up.

3. 3.2 km - You pass a junction with the Evelyn Creek trail (to your right). Ignore this trail and continue on the old fire road.
4. 5.2 km - You arrive at the Bald Hills fire lookout – a great place to take a rest and enjoy the astonishing views of surrounding mountains and valleys. The trail continues for another 2 km, climbing another 150 metres to an even better viewpoint. To continue, look for a sign-posted junction (southerly direction) that indicates the pathway up the elevated ridge. The beauty of the alpine meadows filled with wildflowers will complement your panoramic appreciation as you ascend. Be particularly careful on the rocky areas where it may become very slippery when wet.
5. 6.7 km - You reach the highest viewpoint (2320 m). Enjoy these moments as the views are simply breathtaking. From here, take the same route back. At the junction at the fire lookout, you can decide to take the longer, easier trail back (the way you came), or you can take the shorter, steeper trail (the right trail, the dotted red line on the map).

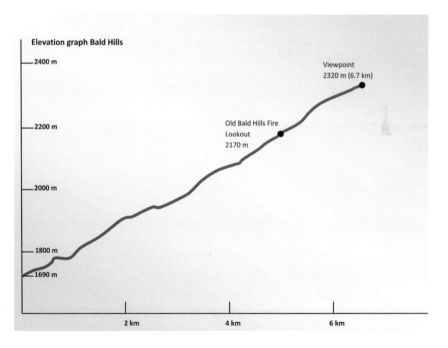

Bald Hills

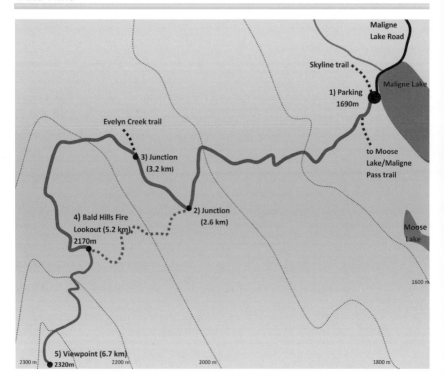

Driving directions

Coming from Jasper, go north on Highway 16. After 2 km, take the exit to the Maligne Lake Road. Cross the Athabasca River and go left at the junction to Maligne Lake Road (north). Continue on the road for 45 km until the road ends at the Maligne Lake parking lot.

29   Opal Hills

ROUND TRIP DISTANCE: 8.2 km
TIME NEEDED: 3 - 4 hrs
ELEVATION GAIN: 460 m
LEVEL: Challenging
PERIOD: mid July - end of September
GEM TREK MAP: Jasper & Maligne Lake

At Opal Hills, you will enjoy the amazing panorama that ranks as one of the top views in Jasper National Park. Looking in the northeast direction from the trail loop, you will see the majestic peak of the Opal Hills rising high at 2810 metres. Alpine wildflowers are most abundant between the end of June and early August and the Opal Hills meadows are a great place to see them. Opal Hills is not really a long hike but it is a steep one. You must overcome 460 metres of elevation in the first 3 km hiking. Just be careful when hiking here on a rainy day. The steep hill may be slippery at various points and potentially dangerous when covered with snow, ice or wet, especially when descending from the summit.

Bald Hills and Opal Hills, two great hikes starting at the west side of Maligne Lake. They are both fantastic hikes. Opal Hill is shorter but steeper. One major difference worth mentioning: when you hike up Bald Hills, you follow the old fire road, easier to walk but not really a natural pathway like the Opal Hills trail.

Opal Hills

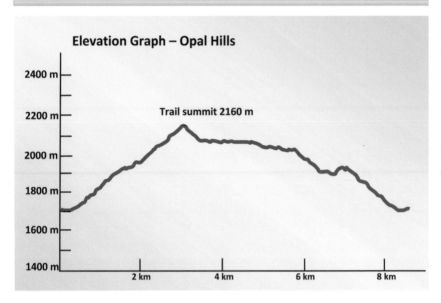

Elevation Graph – Opal Hills

Trail summit 2160 m

2400 m
2200 m
2000 m
1800 m
1600 m
1400 m

2 km   4 km   6 km   8 km

Waypoints

1. The trail starts with a short descend as you walk east. Within 200 metres you pass the junction with the Lake shore trail or Mary Schaffer Loop. (this is the trail to your right). Go left here. Note: The Mary Schaffer Loop is a 3.2 km loop that returns along the lakeshore of Maligne Lake.

2. 1.6 km - You arrive at the Opal Hills loop (junction). The trail on your right is the steeper ascending path. We prefer to take the steeper path up which allows you to descend via the easier, less steep trail (better for your joints and knees). Go right here (counter-clockwise). It is an arduous climb up through the dense forest. You enter the beautiful alpine meadows after approximately 2.6 km.

3. 2.8 km - You arrive at a sign-posted four-way junction. Go left here.

4. 3.0 km - You reach a junction with a trail (right) towards Opal Peak (northeast). Go left here and cross the creek.

5. 3.2 km - You reach the summit of Opal Hills (2160 metres). From here, the trail descends, gradually curving west, then southwest. You cross the creek again before you return (6.7 km) at the start of the Opal Hill loop (waypoint 2 on the map). Turn right at the junction.

6. 8.2 km - You arrive at the parking lot.

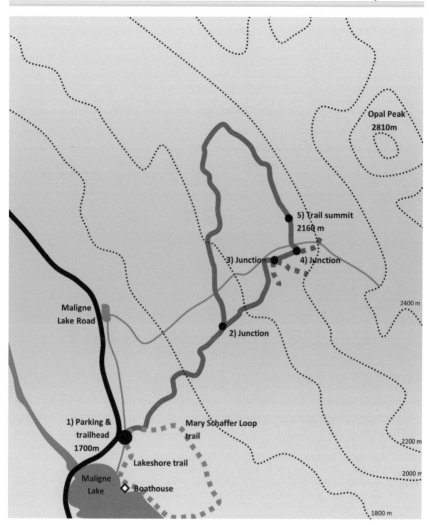

Driving directions

Coming from the town of Jasper drive northeast for about 4 km on Highway 16 and turn right on the Maligne Lake Road. It is approximately a 45 km drive to the end of the Maligne Lake Road where you find the parking lot on your left side. Best is to park your car in the third parking lot (there are parking 3 lots), which is closest to the trailhead.

30   Jacques Lake

ROUND-TRIP DISTANCE: 2nd Summit Lake: 12 km
Jacques Lake: 23 km

TIME NEEDED: 2nd Summit Lake: 3 - 4 hrs
Jacques Lake: 6 - 7 hrs

ELEVATION GAIN: 2nd Summit Lake: 90 m
Jacques Lake: 90 m

LEVEL: 2nd Summit Lake: Moderate
Jacques Lake: Easy

PERIOD: June - end of September

GEM TREK MAP: Jasper and Maligne Lake

This trail is truly unique – ideal for those of you seeking to avoid strenuous hikes with major elevation gain. You only have to walk up and down a few metres in order to arrive at Jacques Lake, 11.5 km from the trailhead. Therefore it is also a perfect day hike choice for young families who may decide to walk only to Beaver Lake (3 to 4 km round-trip). As the trail starts off on an old fire road, it would not be out of the question to reach 1st Summit Lake with a decent baby stroller. This hike is also a good alternative in the early season when many higher level mountain trails are still covered with snow and ice. Beaver Lake is a treasure trove of natural beauty. From the beautiful Medicine Lake (see photo page 124), the trail follows the creek up to Summit Lake. You start in the dense forested lower valley but the views and landscape open up just before you arrive at Beaver Lake.

The feelings of tranquility to be enjoyed along this trail are difficult to match. Beaver Lake, a place loved by bird watchers, is also great for a picnic on a sunny day. From Beaver Lake, you may continue to 2nd Summit Lake which offers beautiful wildflower sceneries. Along the way, you will enjoy the great views on the mountain ranges in the background, like the Queen Elisabeth Ranges in the north - to your right- and the Sirdar Mountain and Colin Ranges northwest. Note that the trail may also be used by bikes.

Jacques Lake

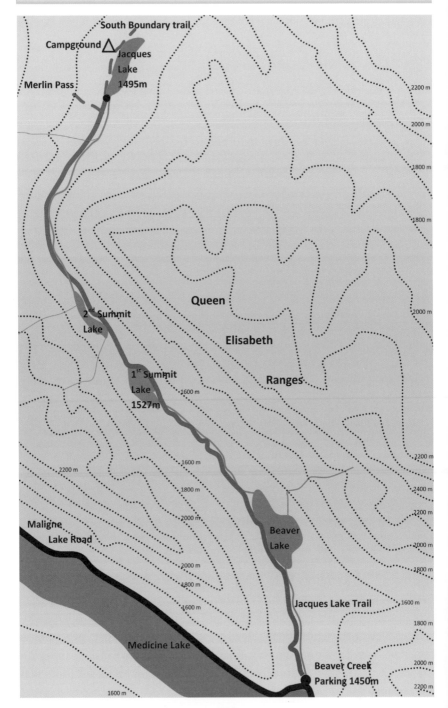

Waypoints

1. From the start of the trail at the Beaver Creek Picnic Area, you follow the creek on its west bank towards Beaver Lake (northwest). Follow the signs for the Jacques Lake trail and the South Boundary trail. *Note: the South Boundary trail is a ten day trail with a total distance of 176 km and it overlaps the Jacques Lake trail at this point.*
2. 1.5 km - You arrive at the south corner of Beaver Lake. Continue walking north on the west side of Beaver Lake.
3. 4.8 km - You arrive at a junction before 1st Summit Lake. Go right, the trail continues (in a north-westerly direction) on the eastside of the 1st Summit Lake. From here to Jacques Lake, you will pass a few streams along your way (depending on the time of the year, they may be dried up). Some areas may be muddy so take care.
4. 6.1 km - You arrive at 2nd Summit Lake. To continue to Jacques Lake, follow the South Boundary trail (north-west). You will again pass some muddy areas and small streams (many will be dried up in the summer).
5. 7.6 km - The trail gradually bends north-east.
6. 11.3 km - You arrive at a junction with the Merlin Pass trail (left). Go straight.
7. 11.5 km - You arrive at the south corner of Jacques Lake (elevation level of 1495m). From here, you can continue walking north along Jacques Lake to the backcountry campground, but for a long day hike this may be your choice to turn around.

Driving directions

Coming from Jasper, take the Maligne Lake Road to Medicine Lake. At the east end of Medicine Lake you find the Beaver Creek picnic area on your left.

31   Maligne Canyon

ROUND-TRIP DISTANCE:	8.8 km
TIME NEEDED:	2 - 3 hrs
ELEVATION GAIN:	110 m
LEVEL:	Very easy
PERIOD:	June - October
GEM TREK MAP:	Jasper & Lake Maligne

Maligne Canyon is a straightforward, well signposted trail and the most impressive limestone canyon in the Canadian Rockies. It is the deepest and narrowest canyon in the park and we present the trail here as it is a perfect adornment to the Canadian Rockies hiking experience exemplifying the striking diversity on offer in this overview of best hikes. It certainly will be a very busy place, but definitely worth visiting. You have a couple of options to see the canyon but the best choice is to park your car at the sixth bridge and from there to complete Trail 7 to the 2nd bridge, where you will have the most impressive views of the canyon. From this point, return the way you came or you can extend your hike with one of the few alternative routes. It is an easy hike through an undulating forested landscape without any arduous climbing (only 110 meters of accumulated elevation gain).

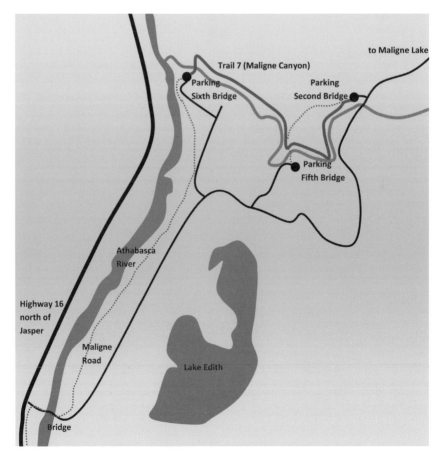

Maligne Canyon

Maligne Canyon

Driving directions

From the town of Jasper, follow the Maligne Lake Road for 2.3 km to the Sixth Bridge Access Road. Turn left. The parking lot is at the end of the road. The trailhead starts on the other side (north side) of the bridge over the Maligne River.

32   Sulphur Skyline

ROUND-TRIP DISTANCE: 9.6 km
TIME NEEDED: 3 - 4 hrs
ELEVATION GAIN: 690 m
LEVEL: Challenging
PERIOD: June - October
GEM TREK MAP: Jasper - Maligne Lake

This is another hike worthwhile to be on top of your to do list. Sulphur Skyline is one of the greatest day hikes in Jasper National Park. Sulphur Skyline can be a fairly busy trail on a nice warm, sunny day, partly because the start of this hike is located at Miette Hot Springs, the warmest natural springs in the Canadian Rockies. The Sulphur Skyline trail is a relatively arduous hike, so ensure you take enough food, water and allow for lots of breaks. The trail brings you up to a mountain top with unobstructed views of the numerous peaks in the area. It is really a wonderful place to hike. On the way up, you may encounter a few bighorn sheep. When you return from the hike, you can soak your muscles in the Miette Hot Springs.

Waypoints

1. The trailhead is located on the right side of the Miette Hot Spring pool. The trail starts with a moderately strenuous ascend.
2. 2.3 km - As the trail narrows, you will arrive at a junction with Shuey Pass. To your left (north) you can see Shuey Mountain. Take a right turn at the junction (follow Sulphur Skyline or Sulphur ridge), and continue on the ascending trail with a few switchbacks.
3. 4.8 km - You reach the summit of the Sulphur Skyline at an elevation level of 2060 metres. On a clear day, the views are superb. You can see the summit of Mount Shuey to the north, the Ashlar Ridge to the north-west and the Fiddle River to the south-east. Take the same route back.

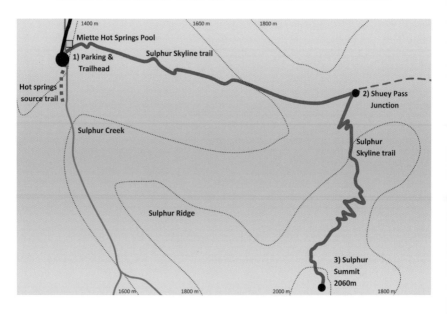

Driving directions

Coming from Jasper, take Highway 16 in northern direction. Take the Pocahontas exit to the Miette Hot Spring Road. Continue for approximately 17 km on this road to the parking lot at Miette Hot Springs.

33   Berg Lake trail to Kinney Lake

ROUND-TRIP DISTANCE: 10 km
TIME NEEDED: 3 hrs
ELEVATION GAIN: 130 m
LEVEL: Easy
PERIOD: end of June - early October
GEM TREK MAP: Mount Robson Park

Mount Robson Provincial Park is the largest Provincial Park in the Canadian Rockies. Mount Robson itself reaches a height of 3954 metres - the highest mountain of the Canadian Rockies.

The Berg Lake trail is the most popular backpacking trail of the Mount Robson Provincial Park and starts southwest of the foot of Mount Robson, ending at Berg Lake just north of Mount Robson. The well-marked trail to Kinney Lake is readily accessible without a difficult elevation gain. The trail winds through an old-growth hemlock and cedar forest as it follows the Robson River. The scenery along this hike is impressive, made up of snow-capped mountains and glaciers, fast flowing streams with waterfalls as well as beautiful canyons and giant trees.

Berg Lake trail to Kinney Lake

Kinney Lake is the first destination of the Berg Lake trail and is a marvellous day hike destination.

The extended trail to Berg Lake (20 km) is a worthwhile trip. You would be well advised to bring your backpack and sleeping gear with you to allow an overnight at the one of the campgrounds around Berg Lake. You can obtain a permit for backcountry camping at the Mount Robson Visitor Centre.

Waypoints

1. You start this hike on a wide roadbed at the Robson River Bridge. After you cross the bridge, the trail follows the Robson River (in a northerly direction) on its north-west bank. You enter a cedar and hemlock forest.

2. 4.5 km - You arrive at the Kinney Lake outlet and must cross another bridge over the Robson River. After the bridge you approach a junction with the Kinney Lake picnic area to your left.

3. 5 km - Continue on the trail along the Kinney Lake shoreline for another 0.5 km (north) for the best viewpoint on Kinney Lake and the surrounding mountain peaks. From here, you can return the same way or continue on the Berg Lake trail which remains an easy walk for the next 4 km. Thereafter the hike becomes somewhat more challenging all the way up to Berg Lake.

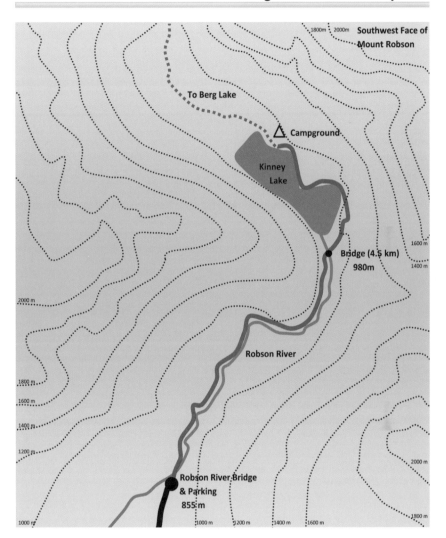

Driving directions

From the Mount Robson Junction pass (Visitor Centre), follow the road (north) for 2 km to the top of Mount Robson junction pass. The trailhead is located on the north end of the parking lot at the Robson River Bridge.